1526 - 1800

FRANK ROBERTS

Hodder & Stoughton
LONDON SYDNEY AUCKLAND

ACKNOWLEDGEMENTS

The publishers would like to thank the following for permission to reproduce copyright illustrations: Cover, Chester Beatty Library, Dublin; Contents, Trustees of the British Museum; p 4 t, Images of India; p 4 b, A F Kersting; p 5 l, Robert Harding Picture Library; p 5 r, Keir Collection, Ham, Surrey; p 6, A F Kersting; p 7, Windsor Castle, Royal Library, © 1992. Her Majesty the Queen; p 8, Michael Holford; p 9 l, British Library; p 9 r, Trustees of the Victoria and Albert Museum; p 10 t, Robert Harding Picture Library; p 10 b, Bodleian Library, Oxford; p 11 t, Chester Beatty Library, Dublin; p 11 b, Royal Academy of Arts Library; p 12, British Library; p 13, Robert Harding Picture Library; p 14, Trustees of the Victoria and Albert Museum; p 16 l, r, Trustees of the Victoria and Albert Museum; p 18 l, Trustees of the Victoria and Albert Museum; p 18 r, Chester Beatty Library, Dublin; p 19 l, Robert Harding Picture Library; p 19 r, J Allan Cash Ltd, p 20, Windsor Castle, Royal Library, © 1992. Her Majesty the Queen; p 21, Robert Harding Picture Library; p 22 l, Trustees of the Victoria and Albert Museum; p 22 r, Trustees of the British Museum; p 23 l, Courtesy of the Freer Gallery of Art, Smithsonian Institute, Washington, D.C.; p 23 r, Chester Beatty Library, Dublin; p 24 l, Bodleian Library, Oxford; p 24 r, Ved Pal Sharma; p 25 l, Windsor Castle, Royal Library, © 1992. Her Majesty the Queen; p 27 t, Historic Royal Palaces/The Tower of London; p 28 l, Biblioteque Nationale, Paris; p 28 r, British Library; p 29, Christina Gasgoigne Photography; p 30, Trustees of the British Museum; p 31, Private Collection; p 32, Ann and Bury Peerless; p 33 r, Trustees of the British Museum; p35, Service Historique de L'Armee de Terre, Ministere de la Defense, Paris; p 37, British Library; p 38 t, b, National Maritime Museum, Greenwich; p 39, National Maritime Museum, Greenwich; p 40, Culpepper Ltd (Herbalists); p 42 l, Chester Beatty Library, Dublin; p 42 r, Yale Center for British Art, Paul Mellon Collection; p 43 t, r, British Library; p 43 l, J Allan Cash Ltd, p 44 l, r, National Army Museum; p 45 l, National Army Museum; p 45 r, b, British Library; p 46 l, Royal Asiatic Society; p 46r, British Library; p 47, Trustees of the British Museum; p 48, Mary Evans Picture Library; p 49, British Library; p 51, National Portrait Gallery; p 53 l, Trustees of the British Museum; p 53 r, Trustees of the Victoria and Albert Museum; p 55 l, British Library; p 55 r, Trustees of the Victoria and Albert Museum; p 56-7, British Library; p 58, Sanjay/AAA Films, Bombay/Channel Four Stills Library; p 59 r, Trustees of the Victoria and Albert Museum; p 60 r, Yale Center for British Art, Paul Mellon Collection; p 61 t, b, r, British Library; p 62 l, The Hulton Picture Company; p 62 r, Popperfoto.

The cover illustration is a Mughal fantasy which shows Emperor Jahangir killing one of his enemies, the Ethiopian General Malik Ambar.

For Jean and Louie, with love and thanks.

British Library Cataloguing in Publication Data
Roberts, Frank
    Past historic: India 1526–1800.
    I. Title
    954.03
    ISBN 0 340 55437 1

First published 1992

© 1992 Frank Roberts

Typeset by Litho Link Limited, Welshpool, Powys, Wales.
Printed in Hong Kong for the educational publishing division of Hodder and Stoughton Ltd, Mill Road, Dunton Green, Sevenoaks, Kent by Colorcraft Ltd.

CONTENTS

Highlighted words are explained in the glossary on page 63.

INDIA AT THE START OF THE 16TH CENTURY

Since ancient times there has been a simple way of explaining what India is: all the land east of the River Indus, west of the River Ganges and south of the Himalaya mountains.

A   Map of India.

This is a huge area of land, bigger than Europe. Millions of people have lived there. There have been many states and governments. The people speak dozens of different languages and have lots of different traditions. But since very ancient times the people there have felt that they belonged to a single   culture   . They were all *Indian*.

The Hindu religion was at the centre of this culture. Hinduism is a *very* ancient religion. It is so old that no one knows who was its founder. There are many different Hindu traditions but there are some things shared by all Hindus.

Hindus are born into a place in society, called their *caste*. They remain in their caste for life. They marry someone from the same caste. They pass their caste on to their children.

There are four main castes — the priests, the warriors, the merchants and the farmers. Your caste decides what job you can take.

Hindus believed that God could take many forms. God could appear as male, like Lord Shiva, or female as Shiva's wife, Parvati. They are both shown in source B.

Sometimes God appeared on earth to right wrongs. There was Lord Rama, who was believed to have been the King of Ayodhya, a city in ancient India.

God could appear as an animal, like Ganesh the elephant god, or Hanuman the monkey king. God could even take the form of a natural object like a mountain or a river. Hindus believed that the River Ganges was a goddess.

C   Sacred cows outside a Hindu temple. Certain animals were very holy for Hindus. Cows were treated with great respect and never killed or eaten.

From around the year 1000 Hinduism had to deal with a challenge from a very different religion, Islam, the Muslim religion. Islam had been founded in the year 622 in Arabia. Its founder was the ` prophet ` Muhammad.

Islam arrived in India in two ways. Muslim armies entered India from the north-west and Muslim traders came to the west coast of India by sea. Hinduism and Islam were as different from each other as it is possible for two religions to be.

Hindus	Muslims
• believed in many gods.	believed in one god.
• had many holy books.	had one holy book, the Qu'ran.
• loved to decorate their temples with pictures and statues of the gods.	believed that it is wrong to have any pictures or statues of God or of other living things.
• are divided into many castes.	are all equal.
• treated cows with religious respect.	thought it was wrong to see animals as holy. They ate cows.

The Muslims who came to India were deeply shocked by Hinduism. It seemed to them that the Hindus were committing the worst sin of all: they were worshipping idols instead of worshipping God. Many Muslims thought it was their duty to go to war against Hinduism and to destroy Hindu temples.

D This statue was damaged by gunfire on the orders of the Emperor Babur. Babur was a Muslim and was very shocked by religious statues, especially *naked* ones.

After centuries of war Muslim rulers set up kingdoms across northern India. Some Indians became Muslims, though most remained Hindus. By the year 1500 there were probably about seven Hindus for every one Muslim.

Many Hindu temples were destroyed. Muslim ` mosques ` were built in their place. Hindus had to pay special taxes that Muslims did not pay.

E Hindus and Muslims did not always meet as enemies. This picture, from about 1600, shows a discussion between a Muslim holy man (left) and a Hindu priest (right). It is clear that their conversation has drawn an interested crowd.

Historical sources provide us with information about what happened in the past. Sources can be written, or they can be pictures like source E.

  1 Explain what a Muslim would have found offensive about sources B, C and D.
  2 Explain why their different beliefs made it difficult for Hindus and Muslims to live together peacefully.
  3 The picture in source E shows a meeting which may not have really taken place. If it did not, why do you think the picture was made?
  4 Source E provides a great deal of historical information. Write down five things which we can learn about India in 1600 from looking closely at this picture.

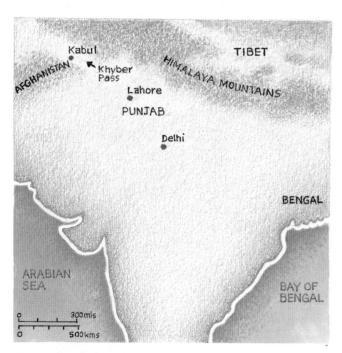

A   Map of northern India.

Across the north and north-east of India lie the Himalaya mountains. These are the highest mountains in the world. Until recent times it was impossible for armies to cross them. Any invading army could only come from one direction – the north-west, down through the Khyber Pass from Afghanistan.

Sometimes India was attacked from the sea, usually from Arabia in the west. But the Arab ships could carry few men, nothing like the numbers in the huge armies which came from the north-west.

What brought invaders to India? India's wealth! In modern times India is not counted as a rich country. This was not always so. India was once famous for its wealth.

B   The first Englishman to visit India, Ralph Fitch, found India far richer than England at that time (1583). In *The Voyage of Mister Ralph Fitch* (1591) he wrote:

The country is very good and beautiful. The streets are the fairest that I ever saw. The goods on sale are gold, silver, rubies, sapphires, musk, frankincense, pepper, tin, lead, copper, rice and sugar.

Fitch's comment is a *primary source*. This means that it was made at the time it describes.

Another traveller from Europe who visited India was Marco Polo, an Italian who was there around the year 1300. He too was impressed by the wealth that he saw.

C   This account is taken from *The Travels of Marco Polo* (written about 1320).

In this kingdom are many mountains in which diamonds are found. In all the world diamonds are found nowhere else but in this country. The country is well-stocked with beasts, including the biggest sheep in the world, and with lots of different things to eat.

Foreign invaders came to India to carry off that wealth for themselves. India also had a huge population. That was another attraction for invaders who sometimes come in search of slaves. India was famous for the skill of its craftsmen. They could make the most valuable slaves of all.

D   This shows the tomb of the Emperor Timur which is in Samarkand in central Asia, far from India. Yet it was built by Indian slaves who were captured by Timur when he invaded India in 1398.

Primary evidence is not always written. Buildings, like Timur's tomb, are also primary evidence.

In 1525 a king from Afghanistan, a descendant of Timur whose name was Mohammed Babur (Mohammed the Tiger) invaded India. Why did he come?

E Babur tells us himself, in the autobiography , *The Baburnama*, which he wrote between 1526 and 1529.

India is vast, full of people and rich. Its best features are that it is a large country, has lots of gold and silver, and there are countless workmen of every profession.

For Indians, Babur's invasion was a terrible disaster. Guru Nanak, who founded the Sikh religion, was alive at the time.

F This extract is from *The Guru Granth Sahib*, written by Guru Nanak.

God subjected India to terror.
The ferocious tiger fell upon a herd of cattle.
Evil strutted around in triumph.
Swarms of women, Hindus and Muslims,
In tatters from head to foot,
Hid in the cremation yards .
The sacred buildings of Hindus and Muslims were burned.
Princes, cut to pieces, wept in their suffering.
Lords of ramparts and forts,
Whose ambition the sky itself
Did not seem to match
Were dragged about with halters through their noses.

Many people thought Babur was just a murdering robber. But he was much more. He made his name in India. The ruling family that he founded, the *Mughals*, ruled northern India for the next 250 years. Many Indians today look back on the age of the Mughal dynasty as a golden age for India.

The Mughals certainly found wealth in India. Source G shows Babur's great-great-grandson, the Emperor Shah Jahan, being weighed. Each birthday the Mughal Emperor gave away to the poor his own weight in gold.

G

1 Explain in your own words why danger usually came to India from the north-west rather than from any other direction.
2 Make a list of all the things which drew foreign invaders to India.
3 Read sources B, C and E.
   a) Are these all primary sources? Give reasons.
   b) Is it true that diamonds are found nowhere else but in India, as Polo wrote? Give a reason.
   c) If it is not true, why might he have said this?
   d) Do the writers agree about the ways in which India was rich?
   e) If they differ, how do they differ?

5 Look as source D. A descendant of Timur, and a descendant of the Indian slaves who built it, might describe this same building in very different ways. Write a description of the building from both points of view.
6 How are the impressions which non-Indians have of India today different from the images which non-Indians had of India 400 years ago?
7 Guru Nanak's account of 1525 (source F) is a poem.
   a) Is it primary or secondary evidence? Explain how you know.
   b) Rewrite what he saw as a story.

People often write autobiographies, telling the stories of their own lives. These can be very useful for finding out about the past. But people might not always tell the full truth or might try to make themselves look better than they were. Keep this in mind when reading the extracts from Babur's autobiography. All the written sources in this chapter are from this book.

A In the year 1525, when the sun was in Sagittarius, I set out on my march to invade India. Great and small, good and bad, servants and no servants, the force numbered twelve thousand men.

This was a tiny force to attack a country of millions. Yet within a year, Babur had conquered northern India.

Who was this man? He had been born 43 years earlier in Ferghana, part of the country we now call Afghanistan. His ancestors had been the great conquerors of Asia: Genghiz Khan and Timur. But Ferghana was not a very important place.

B Ferghana was on the extreme edge of the habitable world, of small extent and surrounded by hills.

And Babur was not a very important king. He became king at the age of 12 after his father died in an accident. He spent his teenage years in a terrible struggle for survival against other rulers. At one time his kingdom was reduced to just one fort and 200 men. Eventually in 1504 he was able to capture Kabul (the main city in Afghanistan) and over the next ten years he made himself the only real king in the country.

C Babur's empire.

In 1525 Babur launched his invasion of India. The ruler of northern India was the Sultan of Delhi, Ibrahim. Ibrahim had an army of 100,000 men and hundreds of war elephants. Yet when the two armies met on 20 April 1526 Babur won a crushing victory. Sultan Ibrahim was killed, along with 20,000 of his men. Babur had won because he had better guns and because the Afghan horsemen were so skilled. Babur's son Humayun then captured the royal city of Agra, and in 1526 Babur became the emperor of northern India.

D Babur dictating his autobiography. A painting from around 1600.

Babur knew that an Afghan king's power over his men depended upon being generous. He now gave away a fortune in wealth which he had looted.

E Every person who had come in the army with me carried off gifts and presents. To the people of my home, to every soul, men and women, slave and free, I sent one silver coin as a gift.

Babur gave away so much that his men nicknamed him Fakir, the beggar. He did not have a very high opinion of his new empire.

F India has few pleasures to recommend it. The people are not handsome. They have no idea of the charms of friendly society. They have no genius, no intelligence, no politeness of manners, no kindness or fellow-feeling . . . no good horses, no good meat, no grapes or musk-melons, no good fruits, no ice or cold water, no good food or bread, no baths or colleges, no candles, no torches, no, not even a candlestick.

Sometimes he missed his home, far away in the north-western mountains.

G How is it possible that the delights of those lands should be erased from my heart? Recently they brought me a musk-melon. While cutting it up I was affected by a strong feeling of loneliness and a sense of exile from my native country. I could not help weeping.

H But then he would remind himself of all that he had won and of the poverty he had left behind. He had this prayer published.
Return a hundred thanks O Babur;
For the bounty of your merciful God
Has given you India and numerous kingdoms,
If unable to stand the heat you long for cold
Remember the frost and cold of your home.

I Timur with four Mughal emperors – going clockwise from Timur they are Humayun, Jahangir, Akbar and Babur. A picture from Jahangir's time.

Babur was a very complicated man. On the one hand, he was a brilliant general who could inspire his men by his speeches. In 1526 he turned the tide in a battle with the Rajputs, a warrior nation of western India, with his words. This is part of what he said.

J With fame, even if I die, I am contented. Let Fame be mine since my body belongs to Death. If we fall we die the death of martyrs , if we survive we rise victorious.

However, he could also be very cruel. When a slave woman and a cook tried to poison him, he had the woman trampled to death by elephants and the cook skinned alive. Yet this same man wrote poems and loved gardening more than anything else.

He made very careful notes about all the plants and animals that he saw on his journeys. In the middle of his invasion of India he found time to write that he had seen 34 different kinds of tulip.

K Babur overseeing the building of a garden.

The questions in this chapter all refer to Babur's autobiography.
_1_ a) This is a primary source. Does that mean that it is always true? Explain your answer.
b) Can you find examples where Babur's own opinions show?
c) Why should a historian always be careful when using evidence from an autobiography?
_2_ Work in pairs. Write two headings, _Good points_ and _Bad points_. In each column, write down what you have learned about Babur from this chapter.
_3_ Do you think that it is possible simply to say that a dead person was entirely good or entirely bad? Explain your answer with examples from this chapter.

HUMAYUN

It was believed that Babur gave his life in exchange for the life of his son Humayun. When Humayun fell ill, Babur was heard to pray aloud: 'Is there any stone which can be weighed against my son? Rather I should pay for his life with mine.' Humayun recovered but Babur fell ill and died. He was 48 years old.

Humayun turned out to be a very weak man and a poor ruler. He was addicted to drink and drugs. He was also very superstitious. For example, on Sundays he would only wear yellow clothes, on Mondays only green clothes, on Tuesdays only red clothes, and so on. Humayun believed it would bring bad luck if he broke these rules.

A lot of Humayun's reign was spent in civil wars and rebellions. In 1542, aged 34, he lost control of the entire empire. He was overthrown by his younger brother, Kamran. Humayun had to run for his life.

With him was his 15-year-old wife, Hamida, who was eight months pregnant. She nearly died crossing the desert of Sind. She was saved when they met a merchant carrying pomegranates, who was able to quench her thirst. On 15 October 1542, in a small desert town, Hamida gave birth to Akbar, who was to be the greatest of all the Mughal emperors.

Akbar did not get a very good start in life. Although Humayun had been able to take a lot of treasure with them, they were homeless. Humayun and his family had to spend three years wandering as exiles in the Middle East, before he was able to get enough support to start winning back Babur's empire.

In 1552 Humayun captured Kamran and punished his brother for the rebellion by having him blinded. To make up for this, he then paid for Kamran to go on a visit to the Muslim holy places in Arabia. It then took Humayun another three years to win back all of Babur's empire.

Humayun died a year later, in 1556. He was on the roof of his palace when he heard the call to evening prayer. On his way down stairs he slipped, fell and broke his skull. Akbar was 300 miles away at the time. Until Akbar returned the death was kept secret and a double impersonated Humayun.

Secondary sources are made long after events by people who did not see them. Some secondary sources are copied from earlier primary sources.

A A painting made around 1700 of Hamida crossing the Sind desert in 1542.

B Akbar wrestling as a child, drawn around 1600.

Akbar was only 13 years old. He had already made a name for himself as a skilful fighter. He fought and won his first public wrestling match just before his third birthday. (Wrestling was a very popular sport with the Mughals.) Another time a murderer got past Akbar's guards. Akbar knocked the man out cold with a single punch. He was also a gifted artist.

On 14 February 1556 Akbar was crowned Great Mughal or Emperor. For the next 250 years most of India was ruled by Babur's descendants, the Mughals. The Great Mughals were:

Babur 1526 to 1530

Humayun 1530 to 1556

Akbar 1556 to 1605

Salim called Jahangir 1605 to 1627

Khurran called Shah Jahan 1627 to 1658

Aurangzeb 1658 to 1707

D This painting was made for Shah Jahan in 1630. It shows Akbar in the centre, Jahangir on the left, and Shah Jahan on the right. Akbar is presenting the crown to Shah Jahan.

C Kamran surrendering to Humayun.

1 a) The scene shown in source D could never really have happened. Explain why. (Clue: look at the dates.)
b) If it never happened, suggest why Shah Jahan had the picture made.
2 Is source A a primary or a secondary source? Give reasons.
3 From the evidence given, find at least three things which caused Humayun to be such a weak ruler.
4 Inside the front cover of this book is a timechart. A timechart lists events in chronological order. It starts with the events which happened earliest and goes on to later events. With each event is the year in which it happened. Make your own timechart of the main events in the lives of Babur and Humayun.

The empire which the Great Mughals ruled was enormous. Akbar's census of 1561 showed 120 large cities and 3,200 towns; each town controlled between 100 and 1,000 villages. In Aurangzeb's reign it was worked out that he ruled 401,567 villages.

No country in Europe was anything like as big as the Mughal empire. Ruling such a big empire was very difficult.

For much of the Mughal period, the map of India below was as good a map as the emperors had. This particular map was a present from King James I of England to the Emperor Jahangir.

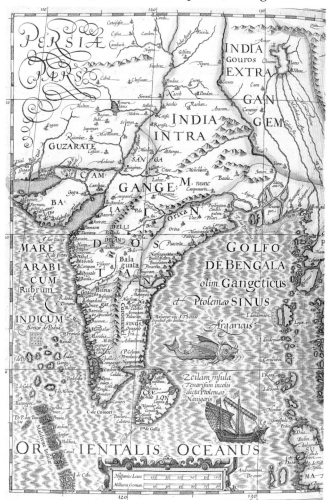

A Mercator's map of India.

At the time of the Mughal empire there were big differences between the rich and the poor. India was, as we have seen, a rich country. Yet there was much terrible poverty and sometimes there were dreadful famines .

B Peter Mundy, an eye-witness of the 1631 famine wrote:

From Surat to Agra, all the highway was lined with dead people, our noses never free from the stink of them. Women were seen to roast their children. A man or woman was no sooner dead than they were cut in pieces to be eaten.

Remember that an eye-witness need not always be telling the full truth. He might add things which he has heard but not seen himself.

People disagreed about what caused the poverty in India's countryside. Babur blamed the backwardness of Indian farmers. Others blamed the empire's officials, who were called zamindars. Some believed that these officials were very corrupt and used their power to build up their own wealth.

C The role of a zamindar as described by a Mr Holwell, who was a zamindar himself in the 1600s:

The zamindar has two jobs, collector of taxes and judge. He has the power of the lash, fine and imprisonment. In all criminal cases [he] proceeds to sentence and punishment immediately after hearing, except where the crime [such as murder] requires the person to be whipped to death.

Having zamindars as both tax collectors and judges caused two problems. It was very difficult to find out if they themselves committed crimes or to punish them if they misused their power.

Emperor   Zamindar

Others blamed the Mughal emperors themselves for being greedy. They said that the emperors were taking all India's wealth to keep themselves in luxury. Even the rich were not safe from them.

D Francisco Pelsaert (a Dutchman who lived at Jahangir's court from 1620 to 1627):

As soon as a lord dies, even before the breath is out of his body, the Emperor's officers are ready on the spot. They make a list of all his property, including everything even to the dresses and jewels of the ladies. The Emperor takes everything for himself, except where the dead person had done good service, where the women and children are given enough to live on but no more.

It was said of Akbar that he was 'Every man's heir' – in other words, when a man died the emperor inherited his goods!

In theory, it was fair to blame the emperor for what went on because every official in the empire was working on his behalf. In fact, the emperor would find it impossible to know what was really going on in so huge an empire.

Mughal justice had a reputation for being strict. Mundy saw towers all over the empire 'made of the heads of rebels and theeves, mortured and plastered in' as a warning.

E An Indian drawing from 1590 of a tower of heads being made.

The Mughal empire was well-run, by the standards of the day. Foreign visitors were impressed.

F Francisco Pelsaert (see source D):

The Emperor's letters to the chief lords and princes are sent at incredible speed. Royal runners are posted in villages 4 or 5 kilometres apart, taking their turns of duty throughout the day and night. They take over a letter immediately on its arrival, run with it to the next village in a breath, and hand it over to another messenger.

So the letter goes steadily on and will travel eighty kilometres between night and day [i.e. roughly 7 km. per hour]. Further the Emperor has pigeons kept everywhere to carry letters in time of need or great urgency. No doubt this is done in Holland but only for short distances, whereas this Emperor possesses the largest area of all the kingdoms in the world.

Akbar even tried to set up a national curriculum for all the schools across his empire. Girls were not educated but he laid down what every boy in the empire should study.

G Morals, arithmetic, agriculture, measurement, geometry, astronomy , physiognomy , logic , household matters, the rules of government, medicine, mathematical and religious science and history.

There is, however, no evidence that these regulations were ever followed in a single school. Most boys never went to school at all.

1 What problems would a Mughal emperor face in running his empire if:
   a) source A were the best map of it that he had;
   b) and source F describes his best form of communication?
   c) Compare source A with the maps on pages 8 and 14. What errors can you see? Pick any one error – what problem would it cause?

2 a) Look carefully at source B. Is there any proof offered by Mundy that he saw cannibalism in India? What does he in fact write?
   b) Does this make him less reliable as a witness?

3 From the evidence in this chapter would you say that there were any benefits for the Indian people in being ruled by the Mughals? Explain your answer.

4 Why was there poverty in Mughal India? Use the sources in your answer.

5 Using the sources in this chapter say what foreigners found (a) most impressive and (b) least impressive about Mughal India.

6 a) How do Akbar's plans for a national curriculum in education compare to your lessons in school?
   b) Suggest reasons why Akbar's plans were never put into effect.

AKBAR – THE GREATEST

1400	1500	1600	1700	1800	1900

Akbar was only 13 when he became emperor in 1556. Right from the start he had to fight to stay in power. There was a rebellion by his troops and Akbar had to fight a battle to recapture Delhi.

He could never afford to forget what had happened to his father, Humayun. Akbar always had to make sure that there was no rebellion inside his new empire.

Akbar spent the years from 1556 to 1560 settling himself into power. He then launched a series of wars which made him the master of northern and central India.

A Akbar once said:

> A king should always be looking for new lands to conquer, otherwise his neighbours will rise in arms against him.

Akbar could not read or write. But we know what he said because he always had a servant with him to write down everything that Akbar said, as he said it. This is an example of a primary source.

B The growth of the Mughal empire under Akbar's rule.

Owning these lands made Akbar one of the two richest men on earth. (The other was Philip II, the King of Spain.)

The biggest threat to Akbar came from the Rajput princes of western India. The Rajputs were Hindus and excellent warriors. Akbar decided that he needed a careful plan. He would offer peace and friendship to those Rajputs who would accept his leadership. He would make war on any who refused.

C The Rajput prince Rao Surjan Hada making peace with Akbar. This painting was made in about 1590.

The artist has painted Akbar showing the prince great respect. Rao is not forced to kneel and is clearly allowed to carry his dagger in Akbar's presence. Any Rajput who saw this painting would see it as a message – that Akbar was willing to trust Rajputs who would trust him.

Akbar wanted to be seen as the lawful ruler of all Indians, whatever their religion. Although he was a Muslim he decided that a Hindu princess would be his chief wife.

In 1563 he stopped the special tax which Hindus had to pay every time they went on a pilgrimage to one of their holy places. The next year he ordered that no one could be forced to pay extra taxes because of their religion.

Many of the top jobs in the army and government were given to Hindus, especially Rajputs. Akbar was not interested in what a man's religion was, as long as he was honest and did his job well.

He wanted the Mughal empire to grow all the time. This meant that it would always be at war. But war with outsiders would stop war breaking out *inside* his empire! Wars with other kingdoms would keep Akbar's relatives and generals very busy. They would not have time to think about trying to turn against him. And if the empire went on growing, there would always be new land for Akbar to give to his relatives and generals to keep them happy.

Religious war was the biggest danger to Akbar's empire. If wars began between the different religions then the empire would fall apart.

Akbar tried to get the different religions in India to talk to each other so that people could find out what they had in common. He built a special building called the Hall of Worship for this purpose. To this place he invited the best speakers and thinkers from the Hindus, Muslims and Sikhs. He contacted the Portuguese in southern India and got them to send Christian missionaries too.

Akbar was not prejudiced in religion. He liked to see the best in each religion. Akbar liked the Hindus' kindness to animals, the religious art of the Christians and the simplicity of Islam. He wanted to stop the violence between different religions which was so common then.

But the religious problems went on. Finally in 1582 he decided to end them by starting his own religion! It was called the Divine Faith. People would worship one God whose representative on earth was Akbar himself. He issued coins bearing the Arabic words ALLUHA AKBAR. These words are a Muslim prayer and mean 'God is greatest'. But they can also be translated 'God is Akbar' because the word Akbar means greatest.

D Alluha Akbar written in Arabic script.

This new religion was not a success. Muslims were shocked by it. Most Indians could not understand it. So everyone except Akbar and his friends ignored it. But Akbar's policy of opening the Mughal empire to all religions went on under his son and grandson. The Mughal empire was strong because it used the talents and strengths of all India's peoples and religions.

1 Explain why Akbar fought so many wars.
2 How does source A help us to understand why Akbar fought so many wars?
3 Why did the painter of source C show the Rajput prince carrying a dagger?
4 In the picture is Akbar being hostile or friendly? Give reasons.
5 Choose three of these words to best describe Akbar's attitude to religion. Then explain your choice: cunning; holy; curious; warlike; tolerant; wise; prejudiced; careful.

AKBAR'S WARS

Sources A and B show an event from one of Akbar's many wars with the Rajputs. They illustrate the siege of the Rajput fort of Ranthambhor in 1569. Notice that both pictures are painted as if the artist were standing near Akbar's troops, facing the fort. This is not an accident. The artist was employed by Akbar. He was painting from Akbar's point of view.

Akbar was determined to win Rajasthan, the Rajput homeland, for his empire. No Muslim had ever beaten the Rajputs. His empire would never be safe while the Rajputs were an independent power.

A   Siege of Ranthambhor I. Painted around 1590.

B   Siege of Ranthambhor II. Painted around 1590.

The Rajputs had a series of well-built and well-defended forts which Akbar had to bring under his control if he was to rule western India.

People thought that the fortress of Ranthambhor could not be captured. It was strongly-built and on top of a mountain.

Source A shows how Akbar built shelters for his cannon and then used the cannon to cause panic within the fort.

Source B shows how Akbar's troops then used oxen to drag more cannon to the top of a nearby hill. From the hill they could bombard Ranthambhor. After a 37-day siege most of the fort was destroyed by cannon fire. Akbar then went in person to talk with the Rajputs. He offered them an honourable surrender and jobs in his army. They accepted and the siege ended.

Akbar's wars with the Rajputs did not always end so well. The previous year, 1568, Akbar had attacked the nearby fort of Chitor. Chitor was defended by 8,000 of the best Rajput troops. They had food supplies to last for several years. The Mughals tried to dig tunnels under Chitor and blow it open with gunpowder. By accident the gunpowder exploded too early and 200 of Akbar's best soldiers were killed. Akbar then built an enormous covered road so that his engineers could safely reach Chitor's walls and undermine them.

C Akbar's friend, Abul Fazl, who was at Chitor, described it:

[It] was wide enough for ten horsemen to ride side by side; high enough for a man on an elephant with a raised spear to ride along it. It had walls of mud and rubble, thick enough to stop cannon balls, and a wooden roof.

Chitor's governor, Prince Jaimal, came down to fight off Akbar's men but was shot dead. Tradition says that Akbar himself fired the fatal bullet but this cannot be proved.

After the prince's death the Rajput warriors launched a suicide attack. They had first killed their own wives and daughters to stop them falling into the hands of the Mughal troops. They then drank opium mixed with alcohol so that they would not feel pain.

When Akbar finally captured the fort he was so angry about the number of his own men who had died that he ordered the massacre of all the people of Chitor. Over 30,000 people were killed. This was not the way Akbar usually behaved and he never committed another brutal act like it.

After the fall of Chitor Akbar made the pilgrimage which led to the building of Fatehpur Sikri, described in the next chapter.

By 1570 Akbar had brought almost all of Rajput India under his control. The Rajputs became a key force in Akbar's army. One Rajput, Man Singh, was even made governor of the Mughals' homeland, Afghanistan.

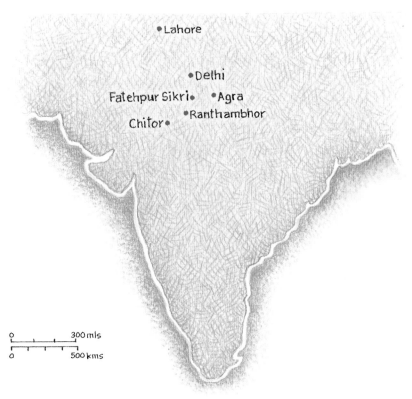

• Lahore

• Delhi

Fatehpur Sikri• • Agra

Chitor•   •Ranthambhor

0   300 mls

0   500 kms

D Map showing the places mentioned in this chapter.

___1 Sources A and B were painted around 20 years after the events they show. Are they still primary sources? Give reasons.

___2 Both pictures tell the story from the Mughal point of view. They might be different if a Rajput artist had painted them. What sort of scenes might one of Akbar's enemies wish to include?

___3 The two sources show a great variety of Mughal and Rajput military equipment. What different weapons are shown and how are they being used?

FATEHPUR SIKRI

By 1568 Akbar still had no son to take over from him when he died. Without an heir the whole Mughal empire might fall apart.

While on a pilgrimage in 1569 Akbar and his Rajput wife, Jodhabai, were staying in the small town of Sikri. A Muslim holy man who lived in Sikri, Salim Chisti, blessed them and said that the queen would soon have a son. Akbar was overjoyed. If the prophecy came true, he swore, he would build the capital of Mughal India on the spot where it was made.

It did come true. In 1569 Akbar's son, later to be the Emperor Jahangir, was born in Sikri. He was originally called Salim after the holy man. And Akbar kept his promise. On the site of the prophecy he began to build his capital, which he called Fatehpur Sikri, City of Victory.

Thousands of architects, labourers, painters, carpenters, craftsmen in glass and metals and textiles were assembled at the site and got to work. In ten years they built one of the most beautiful cities on earth.

At the entrance to the city was a huge arch, 40 metres high, the biggest ever built in India. Across it were some words which Muslims believe were said by Jesus, 'This world is a bridge. Pass over it but do not build your house on it.'

Inside the city were many great palaces. There was the Panch Mahal, the five-storey palace, designed for the women of Akbar's family. It was carefully designed so that they could see out but people outside could not see them.

Another palace was the Hall of Worship where Akbar held his talks with the different religions. Source B, painted around 1590, shows Akbar at these talks. The two figures in black are Christian priests from Portugal.

A Akbar supervising the building of Fatehpur Sikri. Akbar is in white at the top of the picture. Painted around 1590.

The walls of Akbar's palaces were covered with paintings showing scenes from stories about the Hindu gods. This would have been shocking to some strict Muslims. They would have thought that such images were sinful. None of these pictures still exists. They were all vandalised in the reign of Akbar's great-grandson, Aurangzeb, who was a very strict Muslim.

C This Rajput wallpainting comes from the same period as Akbar's palaces. The destroyed pictures were probably very like it.

D Ralph Fitch, an English merchant, saw Fatehpur Sikri just as it was finished. He called it:

A great city, greater than London, with many people.

Although the city was beautiful, it turned out to be impossible to live there. It was too far from any reliable source of water. And so, just 20 years after it was started, Fatehpur Sikri was abandoned. Akbar moved his capital, first to Lahore, then to Agra.

The dry climate did have one good effect. The waterless air perfectly preserved all the buildings. Fatehpur Sikri still stands today, the finest ghost town in the world.

E Fatehpur Sikri as it is today.

All of the Mughal emperors from Babur onwards were famous for their love of beautiful things. They gave lots of encouragement to artists, musicians, architects, writers and creators of beautiful gardens.

Babur himself wrote a magnificent autobiography, *The Baburnama*, full of pictures of his new empire. Akbar had one of the finest libraries in the world. This was despite the fact that he could not read or write. (He had never bothered to learn and said that, anyway, he had servants to do that sort of thing for him!)

Although he could not read, his father Humayun, who was also a talented artist, had given Akbar drawing lessons. Akbar was an expert judge of paintings.

1. In your own words explain (a) how Fatehpur Sikri came to be built and (b) why it was abandoned.
2. a) Describe the sorts of work which are shown in source A.
   b) Give five ways in which it is different from a modern building site.
3. Explain what Akbar was trying to do with his Hall of Faith.
4. Explain why Muslims would not like pictures like source C.
5. Use the information in this chapter to write a description of Fatehpur Sikri as it was in Akbar's time.

MUSIC

Classical Indian music was developed at the Mughal court. Source A shows musicians playing for a new year festival at the court.

It was painted in Jahangir's reign. The musicians are using classical Indian instruments such as the sitar. Classical Indian music consisted mainly of long pieces called ragas. A raga was a short tune upon which the musicians would begin to develop their own musical ideas. The raga could last as long as an hour. Each was carefully chosen to suit the season of the year, the time of day and the mood of the audience.

It was very rare for musicians to play from written music. They learned tunes by heart from their teachers. No two performances were ever the same, as the musicians were free to change the music as they played. And of course nobody was recording the music.

Akbar had the best musicians in India brought to his court to entertain his family, guests and friends. The greatest of these was Miyan Tansen, a sitar player who wrote down about 300 ragas. Tales are still told of the power and skill of the musicians of the Mughal court. One sitar player was said to play such fast, exciting music that objects around him would burst into flame!

Musicians started their training in early childhood. They joined a *gharana* of musicians, which was part family, part school. The pupils had to give complete obedience to their teachers. This included acting as their servants and cooks. They had to practice for about ten hours every day and learn to play hundreds of tunes by heart.

Europeans who visited India found Mughal music strange, but not *very* different from the European music of that time. Ralph Fitch said that he thought Mughal music sounded like bagpipes, but we do not know whether or not Fitch liked the sound of bagpipes. He did complain that Indian music was very loud.

Usually the music was concerned with love, entertainment and dancing. Sometimes it would be religious music. Many Muslims did not approve of religious music. They thought music could make people lazy and sinful. These Muslims thought music had nothing to do with religion. Others disagreed. There was a long tradition among some Indian Muslims that encouraged music. Some Muslims even had dancing at their religious gatherings.

B Sharafuddin Maneri, an Indian Muslim holy man of the 14th century, had written:
To listen properly to religious music you need three things: the right place, time and company. A stone building, clean, tidy, airy and well-lit. The company of friends with taste, able to talk properly. People who are strict with themselves. The time: when one's heart is free of cares and worries.

Akbar tried to make his Hall of Worship fit this description.

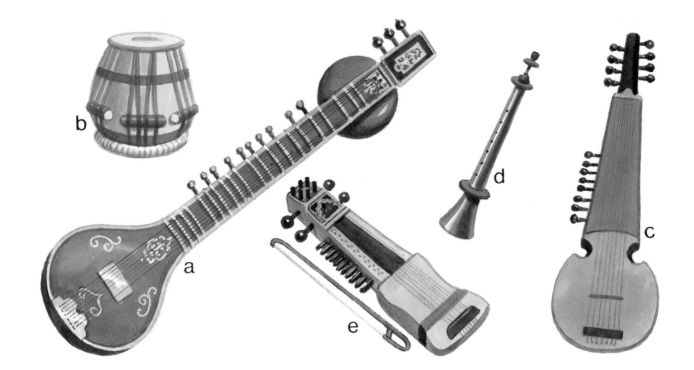

C The main instruments in Mughal music:
(a) the sitar, (b) the tabla hand drum, (c) the
sarod, (d) the shahnai and (e) the sarangi.

The word sitar is Farsi, or Persian (which was the fashionable language in the Mughal court) and means 'three strings'. It was made from a plant called a gourd. Usually, it had six strings which were played and other strings which vibrated as it was played. Early sitars *did* have three strings but, over the years, players added more and more strings. The musicians sat on the floor and plucked the strings like a guitar.

The sarod was brought by the Mughals from their home in Afghanistan. It was like a smaller sitar, but with two gourds. The strings were plucked with a piece of coconut shell.

The shahnai was a double-reed flute. It was a very loud instrument but difficult to play, as it needed powerful lungs and great breath control to make it work. When the Great Mughals appeared in public, dozens of musicians playing shahnais walked in front of them.

Finally there was the sarangi, which was bowed like a small cello. Again, the musician sat on the ground to play.

Classical Mughal music is still very popular in India, alongside modern forms. In this century it has become well known all over the world. Musicians like the sitar player Ravi Shankar and the sarod player Ali Akbar Khan can draw huge crowds in Europe and the USA. Modern singers like Najma Aktar come from a tradition which goes back to the time of Akbar.

D A modern photograph of Indian musicians
playing a classical Mughal raga.

1 Name as many instruments as you can which are being played in (a) source A and (b) source D.
2 a) What problems exist in trying to find out about what music was like at the time of Akbar?
b) Explain how pictures can help the historian in this.

21

Sources A, B and C are examples of a type of painting which was very popular with the Mughal emperors. They are called Mughal miniatures. The artists were not very interested in showing people as they really looked or events as they really happened. They were more interested in producing beautiful images which would please the emperor. The pictures would contain political messages from the emperor to the people who saw them.

Source A shows us the scenes of rejoicing when Akbar's son Salim was born. It was painted around 1590. It was not painted from life. Salim was born in 1569, 20 years before the painting was made. In any case, no artist would have been allowed into the women's quarters to paint the queen and her servants.

The scene is the village of Sikri. In the top left corner we see Jodhabai, Akbar's queen, recovering from the birth while nursemaids look after the baby prince. In the centre people are playing music and feasting. Finally at the bottom of the picture we can see the reactions of various Indian people: there are wealthy men and women, beggars, fakirs and Muslims.

This picture does not exaggerate. Akbar was delighted. It was because of Salim's birth that he started building Fatehpur Sikri as his new capital.

Many ordinary Indians would have been glad, too. If Akbar did not have a son to become emperor after him there could be civil war or a foreign invasion when he died.

When Salim succeeded his father Akbar as emperor he took the title Jahangir. It means 'Seizer of the World'. It shows that he regarded himself as the most powerful and important ruler on earth.

Source B shows the scene at the birth of Timur, the ancestor of all the Mughal emperors. It was painted in 1604, about 14 years after source A and about 250 years after Timur was actually born. You will see that the two pictures are very similar, even though Timur and Salim were born far apart in time and far apart in space: Timur was born in central Asia and Salim about 2,000 kilometres to the south in India.

It was in Jahangir's reign that King James I sent the first-ever English ambassador to India. He was Sir Thomas Roe. He arrived in India in 1615. Roe brought many presents to Jahangir, most of which Jahangir thought were very poor. He did like two of them, an English miniature portrait of a lady, and the map of India shown in chapter 4.

Roe failed to make any real contact with the emperor. For this he blamed Jahangir's chief wife, Nur Jahan. He believed that she disliked him.

A Mughal artist showed Jahangir's attitude to England in this picture.

C Jahangir enthroned, with a mullah , King James I of England and the Sultan of Turkey (1620).

D Sir Thomas Roe wrote in 1616:
All religions are free under Jahangir because Jahangir has no religion himself.

The artist who made this picture tried to make two political points. He wanted to show that Jahangir was not really interested in foreign rulers.

He did not see them as his equals. He also wanted to show that Jahangir was really a good Muslim, who preferred the company of mullahs to that of worldly rulers. This may be because people thought that Jahangir was bored by religion.

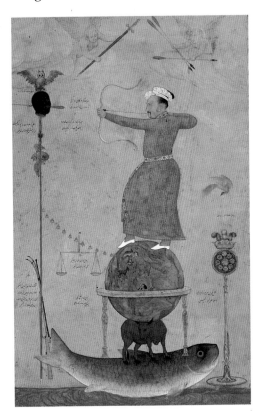

E This Mughal fantasy shows Jahangir killing one of his enemies, the Ethiopian General Malik Ambar. It plays on the name 'Jahangir', meaning 'seizer of the whole world'.

1 In what ways are source A and source B alike?
2 Are there any differences between the two pictures?
3 Source A was painted 20 years after the event it shows.
   a) Could it still be called primary evidence?
   b) For what reasons?
4 Source B was painted over 250 years after the event it shows.
   a) Could it be still called primary evidence?
   b) For what reasons?
5 a) Describe the scenes of celebration in source A.
   b) What sorts of musical instruments are shown?
6 What kind of political point is the artist making by painting the crowd at the bottom of source A?
7 Describe source C in your own words, explaining what it is meant to show. Use source D to explain why it was painted.

Nur Jahan was the chief wife of Jahangir. She came from Iran (then called Persia). They were married when she was a widow of 40. Many people thought that for most of Jahangir's reign Nur Jahan, not the emperor, was the real ruler of the Mughal empire.

A One of many paintings *said* to be of Nur Jahan (18th century).

We do not know what Nur Jahan *really* looked like. No artist was ever allowed to see her and no portrait of her was ever painted from life.

Her original name had been Mehrunissa. Jahangir gave her the titles Nur Mahal ('light of the palace') and Nur Jahan ('light of the world'). There is no doubt that Jahangir was deeply in love with her.

It was most unusual for a Mughal emperor to marry for love. Royal weddings were arranged to link the other royal and noble families of India to the Mughal dynasty. Marriages were made for political reasons. That is why Mughal emperors each had many wives. For example, every time that Akbar made peace with a Rajput prince, he would marry one of the prince's daughters as a sign of friendship. Akbar had over 300 wives.

Nur Jahan wrote poetry, designed fabrics and carpets and ran a business, selling cloth and dye. She often went hunting and had a special closed seat fitted to the back of an elephant, from which she shot arrows. She even took part in a battle. Under her influence Persian clothes, Persian names and the Persian language, Farsi, became the fashion at court. Urdu, the language of modern Pakistan, comes from the mixing of Farsi and Indian languages. Persian miniature paintings were the inspiration for Mughal artists.

Nur Jahan's rise to power also helped her family. Her father and her brother became the chief ministers of Jahangir's government. Her niece eventually became empress after her.

B Nur Jahan was described by Sir Thomas Roe in 1616:

She governs the Emperor Jahangir and winds him up at her pleasure. All justice and politics depends upon her, who is harder to reach than any goddess.

Sir Thomas Roe, the English ambassador, did not like Nur Jahan. He thought she had too much power over the Emperor. He did not think that a woman should have so much power.

A written source may be very hostile to a person and still give useful information to a historian. The historian needs to think about why it is hostile.

Nur Jahan's power was very unusual for an Indian queen. Indian princesses were not supposed to be interested in politics.

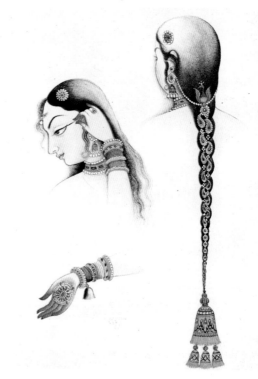

C Make-up and hairdressing in Mughal times.

D New Year celebrations at the Mughal Court, 1645.

Written sources usually deal only with the rich and important. In Mughal India there were few rich, important *women*, so few sources deal with women at all.

The wives and daughters of the Mughal emperors kept the custom of 'purdah' or concealment. Though they were present at court, and often attended important state occasions, they always hid behind special screens. They could see all that happened but others could not see them. The only women who would be seen were servants and dancers. It would have been a disgrace if a stranger had seen the face of a noblewoman.

E This picture, of ladies being entertained by women musicians, gives an idea of how typical Mughal noblewomen lived. Nur Jahan did not usually live like this.

F Sir Thomas Roe described being watched by Jahangir's wives in 1616:
I saw first their fingers, and after laying their faces close, first one eye, now another. If I had no other light, their diamonds and pearls had [been enough] to show them. When I looked up they drew back and were so merry that I supposed they laughed at me.

It was Nur Jahan who arranged that Jahangir's third son, Khurran, was brought forward as heir to the throne. Khurran eventually became Emperor and took the title Shah Jahan. He married Nur Jahan's niece, Arjumand, known as Mumtaz Mahal, which means 'chosen one of the palace'.

Nur Jahan lived for 18 years after Jahangir died in 1627. She went on being one of the most powerful people in India.

1 As Roe disliked Nur Jahan so much, are his comments about her useful for historians writing about her life? Give reasons.
2 Write down two headings, 'Most Indian princesses' and 'Nur Jahan'. Under each write a brief comment on what was typical of each, to show how Nur Jahan was different.
3 There are very few sources from Mughal India which deal with *any* women apart from Mumtaz Mahal. Give two reasons for this.
4 a) What does source E tell us about the sort of life lived by women in Indian royal families?
  b) Give reasons why this would not be the way in which most Indian women lived.
5 From the information in this chapter, what do you think is the social position of the women in source D? Give reasons for your answer.

1400	1500	1600	1700	1800	1900

When people think about the past they often remember only those parts which can be told as exciting or romantic stories. This has happened in the case of Shah Jahan.

Shah Jahan is now remembered above all for his love for his wife, Mumtaz Mahal, who died in 1631. For her he built the world's most beautiful tomb, the Taj Mahal. There is no doubt that this is a most romantic and moving story but a lot more was happening to India in Shah Jahan's reign than a royal love story.

The Mughal empire, which was still enormously rich, was becoming bankrupt. There was no money left. One reason for this was that the empire was now so huge that it was very expensive to run. The bigger it grew, the heavier the running costs became. Another reason was the very luxurious tastes and life-style of the royal family.

A One of Shah Jahan's own ministers wrote:
Shah Jahan's income has increased by 300 per cent since Akbar's time, while spending has increased by 400 per cent.

A lot of this spending was upon jewels. It was estimated that it would have taken an expert 14 years to go through Shah Jahan's collection of precious stones. He had a new throne built, covered with rubies, diamonds, emeralds and pearls. Some Christian priests who visited the emperor were surprised to see that he would ignore his dancing girls and give all his attention to his jewels. One of the jewels owned by Shah Jahan was the Koh-i-Nur diamond. This was the largest diamond in the world. Koh-i-Nur means 'Mountain of Light'. It was later taken by the British and is today one of the Crown Jewels kept in the Tower of London.

After his wife died, Shah Jahan spent a fortune building her tomb, the Taj Mahal. Only the finest (and most expensive) marble was good enough for Mumtaz Mahal.

To make matters worse, the religious troubles, which had ended in Akbar's time, began again. The Muslim religious leaders tried to make Shah Jahan prove that he was a *real* Muslim. They wanted him to stop Akbar's policy of tolerating all religions.

In 1632 Shah Jahan ordered that every new Hindu temple in the empire had to be demolished. In the reign of his son Aurangzeb, the peace between Muslims, Hindus and Sikhs ended completely, and religious wars spread across the Mughal empire.

The empire had never been bigger and it was still growing. But now there were new threats to Mughal power. The Sikhs were becoming powerful in Punjab. In western India the Mughals could not defeat the Maratha leader, Shivaji. There were signs of decline everywhere in the Mughal empire.

SHAH JAHAN HURRIED TO HIS WIFE'S BEDSIDE —

MUMTAZ, MY BELOVED....

MY TIME HAS COME. YOU MUST NOW BE BOTH FATHER AND MOTHER TO OUR CHILDREN. BUILD FOR ME A TOMB SUCH AS THE WORLD HAS NEVER BEFORE SEEN — THAT IS MY LAST WISH.

B

And finally civil war broke out between the Mughals themselves. Shah Jahan's eldest son, the Crown Prince, was Dara Shukoh. He loved reading and study and was not really at home in the world of politics.

Dara Shukoh became a follower of a Muslim mullah, Mian Mir, who wanted to revive Akbar's policy and unite Hindus and Muslims. Dara Shukoh was a friend of many Hindus and even gave gifts to Hindu temples.

This all played straight into the hands of Dara's ambitious younger brother, Aurangzeb. Aurangzeb was a very strict Muslim. He was able to gain the support of many Muslims. Aurangzeb told them that his brother was trying to destroy their religion.

When Shah Jahan fell ill in 1657, civil war began between his sons. Aurangzeb defeated Dara Shukoh and had him beheaded. Aurangzeb then imprisoned his father and in 1659 he had himself made Emperor.

Shah Jahan spent the rest of his life in prison. He was well-treated and his daughter, Jahanara, was allowed to look after him. His great joy was to watch from his window in the fort at Agra as the Taj Mahal was finished.

Shah Jahan died peacefully in 1666. He was buried next to Mumtaz Mahal in the tomb that he had built for her.

SHAH JAHAN BUILT THE EXQUISITE MONUMENT, THE TAJ MAHAL, FOR MUMTAZ. TWENTY THOUSAND MEN WORKED ON IT FOR SEVENTEEN YEARS. THE TAJ MAHAL IS A DREAM IN WHITE MARBLE, THE WORLD'S GREATEST MONUMENT TO TRUE LOVE.

SHAH JAHAN DIED IN 1666 AT THE AGE OF SEVENTY-FOUR. HE WAS BURIED BESIDE HIS BELOVED MUMTAZ MAHAL. **C**

D The Koh-i-Nur diamond is now in the Queen Mother's crown.

Today, when people think of Shah Jahan, it is the romantic side of his story which has been remembered. Many poems, books, songs and films have been made about it. Sources B and C are the final two pages from a recent Indian comic book, which tells Shah Jahan's life story.

Historians try to understand why events happen. They look for causes. In history there are two sorts of causes. There are long-term causes, which go back over many years. And there are short-term causes, in which events are caused by things that happened just a short time before.

An event as big as the decline of the Mughal empire will have many causes.

1 Are sources B and C primary or secondary evidence? Give a reason.
2 What do sources B and C tell us about how Shah Jahan is remembered in India today?
3 This chapter contains several reasons why the Mughal empire began to decline in Shah Jahan's reign.
   a) List as many reasons as you can for the decline of the Mughal empire.
   b) Next, write two headings: 'Long-term causes' and 'Short-term causes'.
   c) Put each of the reasons which you have found under one of the two headings.
   d) Which cause do you think was most important?

1400	1500	1600	1700	1800	1900

People have argued about the Emperor Aurangzeb for centuries. Under his rule, the Mughal empire stopped tolerating all religions. He set out to turn it into a Muslim empire. Hindus and other non-Muslims were fined, removed from government jobs and even executed. Often their temples were destroyed.

Why did he do this? Some said that he was a fanatic , determined to impose his will upon India. But there is some evidence that he was not a fanatic.

A It is believed, though it cannot be proved, that he said:
What connection have earthly affairs with religion? And what right have governments to meddle with bigotry ? You have your religion and I have mine.

Others think that Aurangzeb pretended to be a strict Muslim because his claim to the throne was weak. He had overthrown and imprisoned the real emperor, his father. He had executed his elder brother. Aurangzeb knew that he would be stronger if he could be sure that the Muslim religious leaders would support him.

Aurangzeb was not a modest man. He took the title 'Alamgir' ('Seizer of the Universe'), to be greater than Jahangir ('Seizer of the World'). But he certainly looked the part of a religious Muslim.

C The British ambassador, Sir William Morris, described him as:
All in white, both his clothes and his turban, and his beard as white as they . . . though carried in public he saw nobody, having his eyes fixed upon a book [probably the Qu'ran], reading it all the way.

Whichever is true, Aurangzeb's religious policies led to disastrous wars with the Rajputs, the Sikhs and the Hindu king Shivaji.

Akbar, Jahangir and Shah Jahan loved music. Aurangzeb did not and allowed no music at his court. All the court musicians and dancers were dismissed. They had to look for other employers. As a result they carried the high standards of the Mughal court right across northern India. In fact it helped Indian music.

D A portrait of Aurangzeb reading the Qu'ran, from late in his reign.

The Great Mughals had all loved art. The only art that Aurangzeb liked was architecture, especially building mosques. He had the 'Pearl Mosque' built in Delhi and the Badshahi mosque in Lahore.

B Aurangzeb is presented with Dara Shukoh's head.

E   A modern photograph of the Badshahi mosque in Lahore.

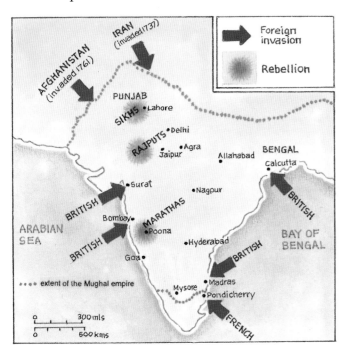

F   The Mughal empire at its biggest in the reign of Aurangzeb.

The Mughal empire had never been bigger than it was under Aurangzeb, yet everywhere there was war and chaos. We can get an idea of Aurangzeb's own feelings in a letter he wrote to one of his sons, Azam, about his top officers.

G   Hammed is a cheat, Siadat and Amin are fools. Zulfikar Khan takes stupid risks. Cheen Khan is worthless, Sirberah Khan is a pickpocket, Muherrim Khan is vicious, Yar Ali Khan is a clown, Arshi Khan is a drunk, Akbar (one of Aurangzeb's own sons) is a tramp, Kambaksh is perverse and takes no notice of anything I say to him. And I myself am lonely and miserable.

It could be said that Aurangzeb had only himself to blame. He trusted nobody. His sons were kept as prisoners for most of their lives. His eldest son, Mohammed Sultan, died aged 37 after 16 years in prison.

Aurangzeb grew worse when his favourite son, Akbar, tried to overthrow him. Akbar was sent to die in exile in Iran. Aurangzeb imprisoned his favourite daughter, Zeb-un-nissa, for 21 years. Her crime was writing letters to Akbar. When Aurangzeb was old and sick he allowed none of his family near him.

Foreigners saw that the Mughal empire was on the brink of disaster.

H   Niccolo Manucci, an Italian doctor at Aurangzeb's court, wrote in 1706:
What an event to behold will be the tragedy following the death of this old man! One only of his seventeen male descendants can succeed and thereby protect his family. All the others will be beheaded or die in other ways.

I   While he was dying Aurangzeb wrote:
I do not know why I am alive or why I came into the world. I have not done well by the country or its people. My life has been wasted. The army is confused and without heart, just as I am. Strange: I brought nothing into the world and now I face God's judgement with a huge weight of sin.

Aurangzeb died in 1707. His worst fears came true. Civil wars broke out, in which two of his sons and three of his grandsons died. The chaos did not end when one son, Bahadur Shah I, won the throne. Over the next 50 years there were eight Mughal emperors. Four were murdered and a fifth was overthrown.

The Mughal empire started to break into separate states. It was so weak that in 1738 it was overwhelmed by an Iranian invasion. By 1784 the Mughal 'emperor' was a prisoner in Delhi. The last of the Mughals, Bahadur Shah II, died in 1862, a prisoner of the British. But the Mughal empire *really* died with Aurangzeb, the last *real* Great Mughal.

___1___ Suggest why Aurangzeb was so afraid of his sons.
___2___ In what ways was Aurangzeb (a) like Akbar, (b) different from Akbar?
___3___ Use the quotations from Aurangzeb to describe his views about the state that the Mughal empire was in.
___4___ Modern Indians are divided about Aurangzeb. From this chapter find reasons why people today might love, hate and even pity him.

SHIVAJI AND THE HINDUS FIGHT BACK

1400	1500	1600	1700	1800	1900

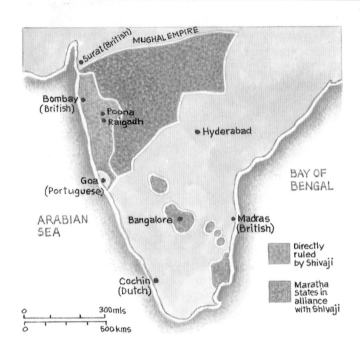

A Map of Shivaji's empire at its greatest extent.

People can become more important after their death than they were in their own lifetimes. We look back at the lives of heroes and heroines as examples for dealing with our own lives. Stories about the dead are passed from one generation to another. People find hope for solving their own problems by thinking about the story of an inspiring person from the past.

Sometimes this can happen simply because people make up or adapt stories about the dead person. But it can also happen when they think about and discuss their hero's life. They may discover more and more meaning and importance in what the hero did and said.

This has happened in the case of the Hindu king Shivaji. For five centuries India's Hindus had been defeated and conquered by Muslims. After Akbar defeated the Rajputs it seemed that no Hindus could withstand the Muslim Mughals. Then, in the reign of Aurangzeb, Shivaji changed all that.

Shivaji was born in 1627 in western India, near the modern city of Bombay. His people, the Marathas, lived on the south-west edge of the Mughal empire.

From the age of 19 Shivaji was at war with the Mughals, first against Shah Jahan, and then against his son Aurangzeb. The Mughal empire was much stronger than the Marathas. So, for much of the time, Shivaji had to fight a war of surprise raids, a guerilla war.

Legends have grown up about this war. Shivaji has been seen as a kind of Hindu Robin Hood: brave, cunning and chivalrous. But these tales were not simply invented.

B Khafi Khan, a Muslim general who fought against Shivaji in Aurangzeb's army, later wrote:

Shivaji went on with his rebellion, robbing caravans and causing trouble, but he never did disgraceful acts. He was always careful to protect Muslim women and children who fell into his hands.

We would expect Shivaji's supporters to praise him. A historian is always interested to know what a man's *enemies* said about him.

By 1666, 20 years of Shivaji's rebellion had worn down the Mughal forces. Shivaji was invited to come to Agra to meet Aurangzeb and discuss peace. He expected that it was a trap but still went.

In Agra he did meet Aurangzeb but he was arrested and not allowed to leave. Shivaji escaped and was able to make his way home to continue the revolt. He was now strong enough to give up guerilla fighting and begin open war.

C An 18th-century portrait of Shivaji.

In 1672 he had a crushing victory over the Mughals at Salher and in 1674 he was strong enough to have himself crowned in the city of Raigadh. He took the ancient Hindu title Chatrapati, or Emperor.

Tens of thousands of Hindus came to the coronation. Nothing like it had happened for hundreds of years. It was also attended by English, Portuguese and Dutch representatives.

Shivaji now set himself up as a rival to Aurangzeb as Emperor of India. European countries began to take an interest in him. The English East India Company prepared an intelligence report on 'Sevagy, the great Rashpoote' (that was a mistake: he was a Maratha, not a Rajput). The Europeans also respected him. He twice captured the British town of Surat and forced the merchants there to give him money. But they noticed that he always avoided killing Christians and refused to allow churches to be harmed.

Shivaji fell ill and died suddenly in 1680. After his death the Mughals tried to recapture the land they had lost. They took back some of it but Shivaji's empire survived. The Maratha state remained strong while the Mughal empire fell apart.

Shivaji's importance has increased since his death. He was the first Hindu for five centuries to defeat India's Muslim rulers. He restored Hindu self-confidence.

D Sir Jadunath Sarkar, a Hindu historian, wrote in 1915, when India was still ruled by Britain:
Shivaji proved by his example that the Hindu race can build a nation, found a state, defeat enemies, run their own defence, protect and promote literature and art, have navies and fleets of their own and fight naval battles on even terms with foreigners. He taught the modern Hindus to rise to the full stature of their growth.

India was ruled by Britain until 1947. Those Indians who wanted India to rule itself looked back to Shivaji as an example to follow.

1 All of the sources praise Shivaji. Why is source B a particularly important statement about him?
2 In Shivaji's lifetime, why would Hindus and Muslims have had very different views about him?
3 Read the two legends about Shivaji (sources F and G). Then list the features of this man which are highlighted by these stories.
4 What does source D tell us about how Shivaji is regarded in India today?

E A modern portrait of Shivaji entitled 'Shivaji Rides Out'.

There are countless legends told today about Shivaji. Here are two of them.

F Sharvaji once received a letter from the famous Hindu saint Ramdas. It contained a poem, some soil, some pebbles and some horse-dung. His mother was angry but Shivaji said, 'No mother, this is the saint's way of telling my future. The soil means the land I shall conquer. The pebbles are the forts I shall take. And the horse-dung means that I shall always have plenty of horsemen to fight by my side.'

G Shivaji went on a visit to the wealthy Sultan of Hyderabad. When he saw the Sultan's magnificent war elephants Shiavji cried 'How wonderful!' 'Don't you have any war elephants?' asked the Sultan in surprise. Shivaji turned to the Maratha troops of his bodyguard and said, 'These are my war elephants!'

A legend is a story which cannot be proved to be true. Legends tell us about the attitudes of the people who believe them. These legends about Shivaji may not be true. However, they do tell us what ordinary Indians believed, and still believe, about this man. For this reason they can help a historian to understand another people's hopes, beliefs and values.

13 THE SIKHS

The 16th century was a troubled time in Punjab, in north-west India. Punjab was always overrun whenever India was invaded from the north-west. It caught the full force of Babur's invasions. In the 16th century Punjab was still mainly Hindu though for centuries the much smaller Muslim minority had held power.

While, in most of India, Hindus and Muslims distrusted and even hated each other, in Punjab some Hindus and some Muslims had found things which both religions shared.

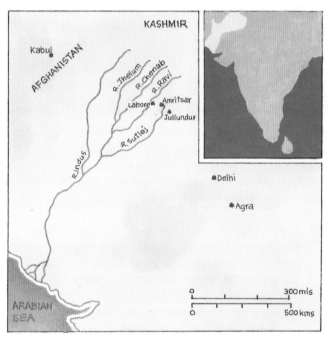

A Punjab – land of the five rivers.

The founder of Sikhism was Nanak, a Hindu born in Punjab in 1469. As a child, Nanak had strong religious experiences. As he grew older, he travelled round India, performing religious songs which he had written. It was not an easy time to be a Punjabi. Nanak saw the horrors of Babur's invasions.

B He wrote:
> This age is like a knife.
> Kings are butchers.
> They give justice only when their palms are crossed with gold.
> Decency and law have vanished.
> Murder is celebrated in song.

Nanak began to preach a message that there was a truth beyond what the Hindus and Muslims believed.

C There is One God.
> His Name is Truth.
> He is the Creator.

He began to attract followers who believed that he was a man of God. They called Nanak *guru*, or teacher; he called them his *sikhs*, or followers. He was still friendly to both Hindus and Muslims. There is a tradition that, when Nanak died, both communities wanted to conduct his funeral. Both saw it as an honour. His portrait may still be seen in many Hindu temples.

D An 18th-century picture of Guru Nanak and the other nine gurus who led the Sikhs after his death.

Guru Nanak passed on the leadership of his community to a series of gurus. It was in the time of the fifth guru, Arjan (1563-1606), that Sikhism began to take shape as a full religion. Arjan stressed that the Sikhs were now a religion in their own right.

E He wrote:
> I do not keep the Hindu or the Muslim fast.
> I serve the One Master who is also called Allah.
> I have broken with the Hindu and the Muslim.
> We are neither Hindus nor Muslims.

Arjan brought together the hymns of Nanak and the other gurus into a book. It was called the *Ardi Granth*, or Holy Book. He also made a point of including the writings of Hindu and Muslim saints. Arjan made Amritsar the Sikh centre. In 1604 the Golden Temple was opened there. It is still the heart of Sikhism.

During Jahangir's reign, the Mughal empire began to attack the Sikhs. Muslims believe that there cannot be another prophet after Muhammad. The Sikh gurus seemed to be calling themselves prophets. Under Akbar this did not matter. He would not harm anyone for their beliefs. For a time Jahangir thought the same. But then he began to suspect the growing political power of the Sikhs. Jahangir executed Arjan.

For the next 70 years the Mughals tried to destroy the Sikhs. Things became much worse for them in 1659 when Aurangzeb became emperor. In 1675 the ninth guru, Tegh Bahadur, was executed by Aurangzeb. His son, Gobind Rai, became the tenth and final Sikh guru.

Gobind decided that the Sikhs could only survive if they were willing to fight a full-scale war against Aurangzeb. He believed that he was called by God to do this.

F Shortly before he died, Gobind wrote in his autobiography:

I came into the world given the duty to uphold the right, to destroy evil and sin, so the good may live and unjust rulers be torn out.

G A modern portrait of Guru Gobind Singh.

On 13 April 1699, on Baisaki, the Punjabi New Year's Day, Gobind gathered all the Sikhs together and from them formed an armed brotherhood called the Kalsa. Only volunteers were accepted.

To show their dedication all would wear special clothes. They would have uncut hair and beards. They would always carry a sword. Each would have the name *Singh*, which means Lion. So Gobind Rai is always called Guru Gobind Singh. Women too could join the Kalsa and would be called *Kaur*, which means princess.

Gobind said that he would be the last guru. After his death the Sikhs were to treat the *Granth*, the Holy Book, as their guru.

Gobind's new army was able to break Mughal power in the Punjab. But before he could set up a government over Punjab, Gobind was murdered in 1708.

H This was painted by an unknown English artist in the early 19th century. It is the first known picture of Sikhs by a European.

In 1799 a Sikh chief, Ranjit Singh, made himself Maharaja of the whole of Punjab. Maharaja Ranjit Singh was a very good general and had one of the finest armies in India.

1 Construct a time chart of the events in this chapter.
2 Which of these statements is the more accurate: (a) 'The Sikhs became a separate community because they wanted to be different' or (b) 'The Sikhs became a separate community because of pressure from the Mughals'? Give reasons for your answer.
3 Source D could not possibly have been painted by one artist from life. Explain why.
4 If you compare source G with the modern portrait of Shivaji in the previous chapter, you will see that they are very similar. What does this tell us about how useful they are as sources of historical information on what both men *really* looked like?
5 There are five things (called the 5 k's) which make up the 'uniform' of a sikh. Find out what they are and describe them.

A
And now the land is close at hand,
The land that so many have longed to reach
The land which lies between the river Ganges,
Sprung from Paradise, and the river Indus.
You have arrived.
The land of endless wealth lies before you.

Camoens wrote 'The Lusiad' to bring glory to his country. It tells the stories of Portugal's explorers. The poem is not very accurate about historical details. It is valuable to historians though because it shows us that in 1570 it felt good to be Portuguese.

These words come from the Portuguese poem 'The Lusiad'. It was written in 1570 by the explorer Luis Camoens. He was writing about the first European ship to reach India. This ship, captained by Vasco da Gama, left Portugal in July 1497. It arrived in the port of Calicut, in south-west India, on 20 May 1498. Few people in India even noticed that it had arrived. No one realised that its arrival was the start of the most dramatic change ever to hit India.

Portugal's ships had patiently explored the coast of Africa. They faced terrible fears and risks. No one knew if you could sail around the southern tip of Africa until Bartolomeu Dias did it in 1487. There were fears that ships would catch fire in the heat or that the sea might boil. Finally da Gama was able to reach India, with the help of an Arab sailor who showed him the way.

The Portuguese did not stop with reaching India. In 1510 they captured the port of Goa and made it their Indian base. Their ships reached Indonesia in 1511. In 1542 they reached Japan. In 1557 they set up a base at Macao in China. At the same time their ships had also sailed west, across the Atlantic, and taken Brazil for Portugal.

The other countries of Europe were bitterly jealous. Almost overnight Portugal had become wealthy and powerful. The biggest threat came from Spain, which also wanted an empire. In 1492 Christopher Columbus had reached and claimed the West Indies for Spain.

To prevent war between Portugal and Spain, in 1494 Pope Alexander VI divided the world between them. All 'newly-discovered' lands would in future belong either to Portugal or to Spain.

B From 'The Lusiad' by Luis Camoens (1570).
We have come across the mighty deep, said da Gama,
Where none have ever sailed before,
In search of India.
Our purpose is to spread the Christian faith.

C How the Pope divided the world.

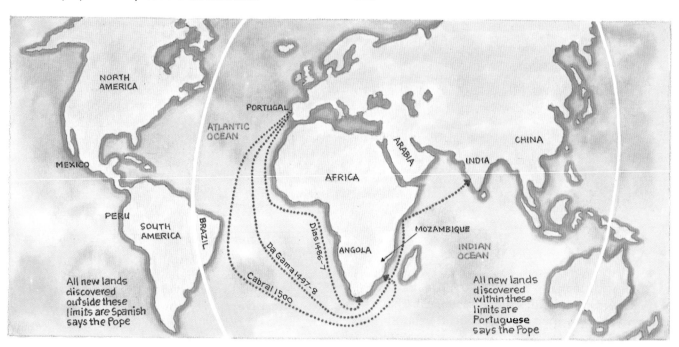

All new lands discovered outside these limits are Spanish says the Pope

All new lands discovered within these limits are Portuguese says the Pope

The Pope was the leader of Europe's Catholics. But many of these, who were not Portuguese or Spanish, were not happy about what the Pope had done. The Catholic King of France, Francis I, refused to accept the Pope's decision. He said that even the Pope did not have the right to divide up the world.

During the 16th century the rulers of England and the Netherlands left the Catholic Church. After this, they took even less notice of the Pope.

The Portuguese tried hard to protect their empire. No Portuguese sailor was allowed to go to work for another country's navy. No Portuguese map-maker could leave Portugal. No Portuguese map could be sold or given to a foreigner.

Anyone who broke these laws faced death. But one atlas was smuggled out to France. After an argument, a Portuguese captain, Ferdinand Magellan, escaped and went to work for the Spaniards. Other Europeans soon found the route to India.

The Spaniards were not very interested in India. They were busy with their rich, new empire in Mexico and Peru. It was the Dutch, the English and the French who followed the Portuguese to India. Over the following 150 years European bases were scattered around India.

While the Mughal empire remained strong, the Europeans would be no real threat to India. Each European ship could carry only a few dozen men. They were no danger to an empire that had an army of over one million soldiers.

But after Aurangzeb died in 1707, the Europeans got their chance. Civil wars began between Aurangzeb's sons and the Mughal empire fell apart into smaller states. Some Indian rulers even invited European armies in to help them fight wars against other Indians. It was easy to bring the Europeans in. It was going to be a lot harder to get rid of them.

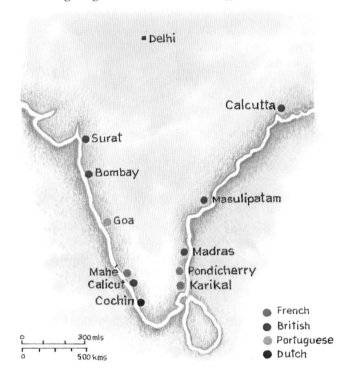

E European bases in India by the 18th century.

D A page from the smuggled atlas.

Early map-makers had to fill their maps with pretty pictures like these because they did not have enough real information to put in. But the ship *is* a genuine picture of a Portugese caravel.

____1 In sources A and B Camoens gives two different reasons why the Portuguese went to India. What are they?
____2 You will need a modern atlas to answer this question. Under the Pope's division of the world, would the places listed below go to Spain or to Portugal:
(a) Japan? (b) Florida? (c) California? (d) Canada? (e) Sri Lanka?
____3 It is 1570. You are interviewing Luis Camoens about why he is so proud of his country. What would he say?

THE EAST INDIA COMPANY

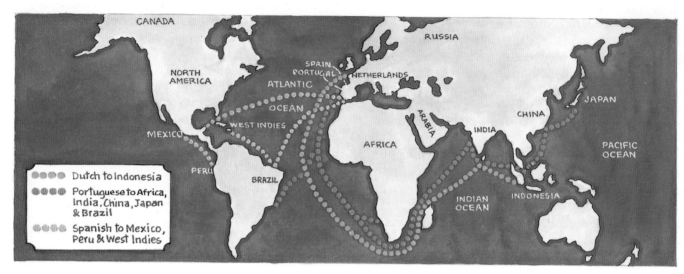

A   Map of sea routes.

Since the late 1400s European countries such as Spain, Portugal and the Netherlands had been winning overseas empires for themselves. They wanted to own the wealth of the non-European countries. They wanted to control the supply of valuable goods like gold, silver, opium, sugar and spices which could not easily be bought in Europe.

The English had been slow at building an empire for themselves. By the end of the 1500s most of the world's sea routes were firmly in the control of the Spanish, Portuguese and Dutch.

Yet the English had begun to make some progress. Those Englishmen who wanted to make real wealth from overseas trade knew that India was the one country they had to reach. A few Englishmen like Ralph Fitch had already been there. And India's wealth had been a legend for centuries.

In January 1601 five small ships left England for India. Fifteen months later they arrived in India. These ships were the first ever sent to India from England. They belonged to a new company which had just received its charter from Queen Elizabeth I. It was the only English company allowed to trade with India. The Company was called the London East India Company.

The men who set up the company were mainly London businessmen. They each put in a sum of money, called an investment. If the ships brought valuable goods back from India they would make a profit. The more money you had invested in the first place, the bigger was your share of the profit. Their investment was a wise one. Over the next two centuries the Company made profits of at least 8 per cent every year.

Life in the East India Company was not easy. Its employees had long contracts, for at least five years' work. Many left England as young men and never returned. Of the first 3,000 Englishmen to go to India, it is reckoned that 2,000 never came back. Others were away from Britain for their entire working lives.

B   One young man in the early 18th century wrote:

> At home men are famous for doing nothing; here they are famous for their hard work. At home is respect and reward; abroad disrespect and heartbreaking. At home is content; abroad grief, cares and displeasure.

But there was never any shortage of volunteers.

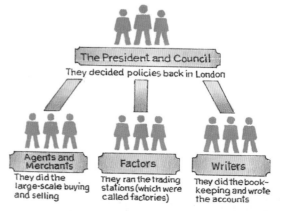

The Company had a very strict chain of command.

The East India Company was in some ways very different from a modern firm. It had its own army and navy for example. It needed these. If there was trouble with another company, or its customers, or the Mughal empire, it could not go to the courts or to the police. English law was thousands of miles away. Problems had to be settled there and then, in India, by force. If they wanted to stay in business, the East India Company's employees had to learn to be soldiers as well as businessmen.

The safest way to stay successful was to have an area of India that the Company directly owned and controlled. The Portuguese had already set the example, when they took Goa by force.

In 1613 Jahangir allowed the East India Company to set up a trading station, known as a factory, at Surat. This was Britain's first step into owning land in India.

In 1640 the company was allowed to set up a factory just outside the Mughal empire, on the south-east coast. Originally called Fort St George, it grew into the city of Madras.

Bombay, in western India, belonged to Portugal. (Bombay means good harbour in Portuguese.) The Portuguese had never made much use of it because it was so near Goa. King Charles II of England was given Bombay as a wedding present by his father-in-law, the King of Portugal, when he married a Portuguese princess.

In 1668 Charles rented Bombay to the East India Company for £10 a year. The Company made Bombay their headquarters in India. It was not long before Bombay was taking business away from Goa. Today, Bombay is the richest city in India.

In the 1680s Aurangzeb tried to force the British out of India. He realised that the Europeans were now becoming a threat. British factories were attacked. But the British navy was able to persuade Aurangzeb to think again. British ships could stop Muslim pilgrims from sailing to the Muslim holy places in Arabia. As a good Muslim, this worried Aurangzeb a lot.

A deal was done. In 1690, in return for paying a fine of £17,000, the Company was allowed to continue. The deal included the right to build a new factory in Bengal, the richest part of the Mughal empire.

It was built in 1696. Its official name was Fort William, after the king at that time, William III. But it became known by the name of a nearby temple, or *ghat*, dedicated to the Hindu goddess Kali Ma – Kalighat, or Calcutta.

Surat, Madras, Bombay, Calcutta: these four cities were the seeds from which British rule in India grew.

---

1   How true is each of these statements? (Give evidence from the chapter.)
a) The British went to India to spread Christianity.
b) The British went to India to make money from trade.
c) The British went to India in order to explore.
d) The British went to India to conquer land.
e) The British went to India because they wanted to keep up with other European countries.

2   It is 1600. (a) You are a London businessman who has just put £200 into the new East India Company. (b) You are a young man who has decided to join the East India Company as a writer. For each, write a letter to a friend explaining why you have done this and what you hope to get out of it.

C   A painting of Bombay as it was in 1732.

THE SHIPS OF THE EAST INDIA COMPANY

The sea journey from Britain to India was long and dangerous. Pirates often attacked ships. They might be attacked by ships from other countries, like France. Ships were often sunk by storms. East India Company ships had to be strong, fast and well-armed.

A typical East Indiaman, as the ships were called, was 30 metres long and 10 metres wide. Those built in England were made of oak. Most were built in India, of teak, the finest shipbuilding wood in the world. A ship usually carried three masts, each with up to five sails. All carried guns, usually 30.

A typical ship had 120 men, including officers. Officers wore uniforms. The sailors had no special dress but wore a style of clothes which marked them out from ordinary people.

A A ship's plan and painting of *The Falmouth*, an East Indiaman.

A SECTION and PLAN of the FALMOUTH Built at BLACKWALL Anno 1752

B 'Saturday night at sea', by George Cruikshank, late 18th century. The men in this picture show what a typical sailor looked like – striped jerseys, with canvas trousers and tarred hair.

An Interesting scene, onboard an East-Indiaman, showing the Effects of a heavy Lurch, - after dinner. -

Pub.d Nov.r 9th 1818 by G Humphrey 27 St James's St.r London -

Crews were away at sea for months. They had to be able to support themselves in an emergency. Every ship had to include men with special skills. There would be a carpenter, a surgeon, a gunner, a cook, a sailmaker, a clerk, a cooper (to make barrels) and sometimes even a butcher. At time of war there would be soldiers too. These were called marines.

As well as the captain, there were usually six officers and six mates. These were directly employed by the East India Company. The officers had to *buy* their jobs! A captain's job could cost him £10,000. It was worth paying so much. Officers could make lots of extra money from each voyage. They could charge any passengers whatever they liked. Warren Hastings' wife had to pay £5,000 to sail back to England in 1785. The captain of her ship kept all of it.

Officers were also allowed to carry their own goods to sell in England or India. It has been worked out that between 1785 and 1793 the Company's officers made over £6 million from selling their own goods.

Ordinary sailors were paid a lot less. They earned about £1.25 a month. This was the same as the pay of a skilled workman back in London. Pay did improve during wars. The Royal Navy would want to recruit experienced sailors. The

C Passengers aboard an East Indiaman, drawn by Cruikshank in the late 18th century.

Company then had to raise wages to keep its crews. Pay could go as high as £3.50 per month.

It was not a pleasant life on an East Indiaman. Discipline was very strict. A sailor who caused trouble might be left behind on a desert island. Sailors were often flogged with a whip. Disease was common. Crews often spent years away from home. The East India Company always had trouble getting enough sailors. From early days it employed Indian and Chinese sailors too.

Cruikshank was a cartoonist and drew to make people laugh. But he had been on an East Indiaman and knew what it was like.

___1___ How reliable as evidence do you think the two pictures by Cruikshank (sources B and C) are? Give reasons.

___2___ a) Write a letter home from a sailor on an East Indiaman, describing what life is like on your ship.
b) Then write an advertisement for an 18th-century newspaper to try and attract passengers to sail to India.

THE VOYAGE OF THE *HEATHCOTE*

We can get a very clear idea of what was involved in sailing on the ships of the East India Company if we look closely at one particular voyage by one particular ship.

The *Heathcote* was a typical 18th-century East Indiaman. In 1730 the East India Company decided to send the *Heathcote* from London to Bombay, by way of the Middle East. The captain was told to call at the Arab port of Mocha, to buy a cargo of coffee. Coffee was a fashionable new drink in London. It was very expensive to buy but very profitable for the seller. The captain was David Wilkie. His job was to see that the voyage went safely. The business part of the voyage was organised by the East India Company's representative on board. His title was the Supracargo, and his name was John Starke.

The Company always gave detailed 'Written Instructions' to its officers. It wanted them to know exactly what they had to do. What follows comes from the 'Written Instructions' given to Captain Wilkie and Supracargo Starke. (The original spelling has been used in these sources. Some words are in italics. These are explained at the end of the chapter.)

This was to be the *Heathcote's* final voyage for the Company before it was sold. Altogether it made four voyages to India between 1720 and 1730. The *Heathcote* had a safe and prosperous journey.

B Aloes.

A

Coffee is the chief *commodity* we expect to have returned to us. If you meet with any good *Aloes* at reasonable price buy, and load as far as 10 tons.

We have sent by this ship 40 bales of broadcloth which we cannot doubt you will be able to sell for a reasonable profit. Also 10 tons of English copper for a tryal.

Remember to weigh every bale, because the camel drivers are always ready to pilfer what they can. If you catch any pilfering, do your utmost to get the fellows punisht, to detere them and all others for the future.

Do not trust the merchants of other natives with your *pieces of eight*.

We have reason to believe that some Pirates may be abroad in the East Indies or lying off the Cape of Good Hope. They took two ships and attached a third.

Put your ship in a good *posture of defence*. Be very watchful at all times and cautious of speaking to any ship. Keep a good look-out during the whole voyage.

We empower you, in case you are in danger of being attack'd by Pirates, to promise your ship's company a *gratuity* of 2 chests of our ship's treasure.

We are having great reason to believe that some of our Captains, while they were in India, have disposed of parts of their ships' *ordinances*. We positively forbid you to sell or part with any gun.

Keep all your *mariners* and all the English in your power in due bounds of *sobriety* and civil behaviour when any are ashore. Suffer no riotous disorder.

We strictly direct you that you do not open any cask of strong liquor under any of the decks. Whenever any cask is to be opened bring it upon the Upper Deck. If you do otherwise we shall deeply resent and punish it.

We strictly require you to keep up the worship of God on your ship and good order amongst your men, taking good care of their Healths during the whole voyage.

We observe that several French and other Europeans have deserted their ships and factorys and turn'd *mahometan*, from whence inconvenience, and therefore you must be very vigilant to prevent the like happening to you, which would obstruct and prejudice our affairs and be a great scandal to the Christian Religion.

We positively forbid you and all officers and ship's company *running* any goods whatever on pretence of saving the Customs due to the government.

You are not to put into Plymouth or any port of England or Ireland or Europe except in case of unavoidable danger.

Keep diaries of all your proceedings. Send an account of *all material occurances* and *transactions* during your voyage.

We are your loving friends
Mathew Decker Chairman
Josias Wordsworth Deputy
London
the 4th Novem 1730

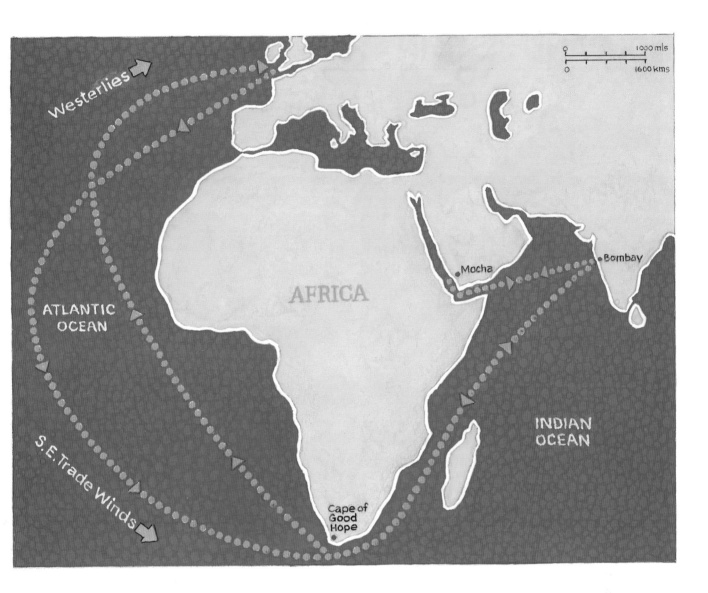

C Route taken by the Heathcote.

Glossary of words in this chapter:

commodity anything which can be bought or sold

aloes a plant used in medicine and in the manufacture of perfumes

pieces of eight gold coins

posture of defence on guard to protect

gratuity gift

ordinances cannon

mariners sailors

sobriety the opposite of drunkenness

mahometan Muslim

running smuggling

all material occurances everything important that happens

transactions buying and selling

Work in pairs.

__1__ a) The paragraphs in source A come straight from the handwritten records of the East India Company. Are they primary or secondary sources? Give reasons.

b) What was the purpose of this voyage?

c) What steps were ordered to avoid the ship being attacked by pirates?

__2__ Decker and Wordsworth mention offering the crew treasure if they were attacked by pirates. What do you think would be the point of this?

__3__ What does this source tell us about the attitudes of the Company's officials towards the people with whom they traded in the East? Give examples.

__4__ There is evidence that some criminal activities had been going on in recent East India Company voyages. List the possible crimes and the evidence for them hidden in the source.

__5__ Why do you think that there are such strict controls on opening the barrels of strong drink?

__6__ How does this source help us to understand what life was like on an East India Company ship?

Source A seems to show a European man meeting an Indian prince. It does not. The 'European man' is in fact an Indian dancing-girl, dressed in European male clothes, as part of an entertainment for the prince. The painting was made in about 1670 and suggests that the Indians still thought that the clothes and manners of the English were funny.

Both the English and the Indians found things which were strange, attractive, comic and shocking about each other's customs and ways. There was a big demand in both countries for pictures showing the odd ways of the foreigners.

English men were very intrigued by the Indian dancing girls, such as the one shown in source B. There was nothing quite like these women in England. These girls were often well-educated and had a respected and traditional place in Indian culture.

This picture, painted by an English artist, concentrates upon the features that would have seemed most strange to the English. There is the Indian jewelry worn on the face, and the water-cooled hookah pipe.

One feature of Indian life which angered many people in England was the Hindu practice called sati (usually spelled 'suttee' at that time). For centuries it had been the custom among Hindu warrior nations, like the Rajputs, for a widow to sacrifice herself by lying next to her husband and

B Indian dancing girl, painted 1772.

being cremated with him. This was regarded as the most brave, honourable and fitting way for a woman to die.

The officials of the East India Company refused to ban sati in those parts of India that they controlled. They knew that sati was honoured by India's Hindu warriors. People back in England thought that the Company's officials were un-Christian cowards.

However, in the late 18th century some Englishmen did respect Indian culture. In 1785 Charles Wilkins, an official of the East India Company, published the first English translation of the Hindu holy book, the *Bhagavad Gita*.

THE BURNING SYSTEM ILLUSTRATED.

C This is a cartoon by Thomas Rowlandson, dated 1815. It mocks the cowardice of the East India Company for not banning sati.

D In his introduction to the *Bhagavad Gita* Wilkins wrote:

> It is not very long since the inhabitants of India were considered little better than savage. But their writings will survive when British rule in India has long ceased to exist.

The British were also fascinated by Indian architecture. When the Prince Regent, later to be King George IV, wanted to build a fashionable place of entertainment at Brighton, he tried to build something as near as possible to the palaces of the Mughal emperors.

E The Royal Pavilion at Brighton, built between 1784 and 1827.

Source F shows that a balance was finally struck between English and Indian suspicion of each other. It shows English soldiers in 1843 bringing their regimental flags to a Hindu priest to be blessed. It is important to notice that both the English officers thought this worthwhile and that the priest agreed to do it.

F

1 What evidence is there in this chapter for each of the following statements?
   a) The British and the Indians found each other funny.
   b) The Indians and the British hated each other.
   c) The British and the Indians were fascinated by each other.
   d) The Indians and British gradually came to respect each other.
2 The East India Company refused to ban sati. Was this because of: (a) religion; (b) respect; (c) politics? Give reasons.
3 In what way does the building in source E look Indian?

A Sir Thomas Roe, the English ambassador at the time of Jahangir, wrote:

I took a view of the Mughal's camp, one of the greatest wonders I ever beheld. It was no less than 20 English miles across.

The army of the Mughal empire had been huge. The camp had contained something like one million soldiers. The backbone of the Mughal army was the cavalry, or horse soldiers. Few of these had come from Afghanistan with the original Mughals. They were mainly recruited from the Indian warrior   nobility , such as the Rajputs.

The British and French went on recruiting most of their soldiers in India. Europe was simply too far away. Many European soldiers fell ill and died in the Indian climate. So the European empires in India were mainly won and defended by Indian troops. This was not as strange as it might sound. Most of the European soldiers in the army of the *English* East India Company were Irish and Scots, not English.

It was not hard to find soldiers in eighteenth-century India. As the country became poorer, soldiering was as least regular and well-paid work.

In 1756 the East India Company decided that its footsoldiers would wear British-style uniforms.

B The Company had two reasons:

It will give them a more military appearance and take off the market a considerable quantity of woollen goods [which the E.I.C. was unable to sell].

C

The troops shown in source C are foot soldiers of the British army, also called infantry. Unlike the Mughal empire's army, the armies of the East India Company were mainly infantry. Most of the soldiers had once been peasant farmers. These Indian footsoldiers were called *sepoys*.

D A sepoy had to swear an oath when he joined the East India Company's army:

I do swear to serve the Honourable Company faithfully against all their enemies, while I continue to receive their pay and eat their salt. I swear to obey orders, never to abandon my post or forsake the   colours , or to turn my back on the enemy. I will in all things behave like a good and faithful sepoy.

He also had to swear to give a month's notice before leaving the army, and promise that when he left he would give back his rifle.

Cavalry were most likely to wear Indian clothes, the sorts of uniforms that had been used in Mughal times. The cavalry were elite 'shock' troops. A lot of time and money went into their training. They were very expensive to equip. Their horses had to be specially brought from Arabia, and were the best in India. Cavalrymen were meant to look impressive. It added to the impact of a cavalry charge.

E One of Skinner's Horse at training, 1840.

James Skinner was the son of a Scottish man and a Rajput princess. At first he fought against the British, both for the French and for Indian rulers. After the victories of the British in the 1790s he joined them and set up a cavalry force known as Skinner's Horse. Skinner recruited large numbers of troops from the Mughal and Rajput armies into this force, as these were the best horsemen in India. They went on using the uniforms worn in the Mughal and Rajput armies.

F The Battle of Nagpore, 1817.

Source F is one version of what an 18th-century battle would have looked like. It is meant to show the British as orderly and the Indians as a mob. There are few pictures of battles from that time which were not trying to show that one side was better than the other.

There are war elephants in source F. These played an important part in battle. They could

G Cavalry charge of Maratha troops in the British army, 1791.

terrify enemy troops. They could smash through enemy lines, like tanks in modern wars.

War elephants were a risky weapon though, if they became frightened. An elephant that was trying to run away could cause terrible damage to its own side.

The officers of the East India Company's army were always either European or, as in the case of Skinner, partly European. There were no Indian officers. Many of the British soldiers had a reputation for being lazy and unsoldierly.

Source H is meant to be an exaggeration. But it does show the common image of the officers of the E.I.C.'s army. The two young gentlemen seated are officers.

H Receiving a report – a cartoon published in 1843.

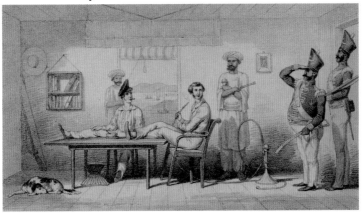

1 Explain the meaning of these words:
(a) sepoy and (b) cavalry.

2 If you were an Indian farmer who had just joined the British army, what reasons could you give for joining a foreign army?

3 Suggest reasons why there were no Indian officers in the army of the East India Company.

4 How would a general have used (a) cavalry and (b) elephants in a battle?

5 Compare the charges shown in sources F and G. Which do you think is the more realistic picture? Give reasons.

6 a) Describe the officers shown in source H.
b) What points is the artist trying to make?

WHAT HAPPENED TO INDIA'S WEALTH?

The British traders of the East India Company came to India because of its fabulous wealth. Many of them made great fortunes while they were there. But, as we shall see, India did not benefit from the rule of the E.I.C. For many Indians the 18th and early 19th centuries were disasters. India's own industries collapsed.

India had its traditional industries. The most important of these were the production of the very fine-quality cotton cloths called muslin, and the manufacture of carpets.

Indian cloth was in such demand that it threatened to destroy England's own textile industry. So, in 1700, a law was passed by Parliament in London. It became illegal to import Indian cloth into England and Wales. English cotton manufacturers then copied Indian textiles and sold them, both in England and throughout the British Empire.

Source A shows the traditional methods which were still in use in the Indian textile trade even in the late 19th century. At the same time the English cotton industry had long completed its industrial revolution.

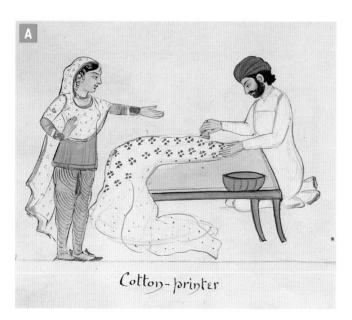

Cotton-printer

Over the next century the English cotton industry became the most advanced in the world. By the time that the East India Company had conquered Bengal, English cotton was being exported to India in large quantities.

The value of British cotton exports to India was £1.2m in 1786, and £18.4m by 1809.

The English could buy their cotton cheaply from America. They could bleach and dye the cloth using the very latest chemical discoveries like chlorine. They had steam-driven power looms.

There was simply no way in which Indian textile workers could compete with this. The new imported English cotton cloth was far cheaper than anything which could be made in India. It was cheap because it was made by machine, not by hand. Imports from Britain destroyed the Indian cotton industry and caused thousands of Indian textile workers to starve.

Source B is another view of traditional Indian craftsmanship. It shows the Muslim prophet Idris. According to legend, Idris was the inventor of weaving. The picture shows him setting up the first Indian textile industry. This Mughal picture was painted around 1600 and shows the state of the art of weaving before the British arrived.

C This picture is entitled 'The East Offering its Riches to Britannia'. It was painted in 1778 and covered one of the ceilings in the headquarters of the East India Company. It shows a British view of relations between Britain and India. This painting was done shortly after the British conquest of Bengal.

D The modern Bengali historian R. C. Majumdar has worked out that:

The total drain of wealth from Bengal to Britain between 1757 and 1780 amounted to £38 million pounds.

British rule brought the products of modern industry to India. At the same time it destroyed India's own industries. The same process brought both good and harm.

1 a) Who benefited from the destruction of India's textile industry?
b) How did they benefit?
c) Would the British have seen what happened to India as progress? Give reasons.
d) Would the Indians have thought that it was progress?
e) What does this tell us about the difficulty of using the idea of progress in talking about the past?

2 a) Look closely at source C. Decide which number best fits each description below:
 • Britannia (symbol of Britain) seated on lions;
 • Neptune, the Roman god of the sea;
 • Mercury, the Roman god of merchants and thieves, who carries a curved stick;
 • a ship of the East India Company.
b) Then explain what is going on in the picture.

3 a) What does source C tell us about British attitudes to India in the 18th century?
b) How would source C have been seen by Indians?

ROBERT CLIVE AND BENGAL

If one man set the British on the path to being rulers of India it was Robert Clive. Clive had a strong sense of his own importance. When he was 17 years old and new to India he was so bored and lonely that he tried to kill himself. Twice he put a loaded gun to his head and twice it failed to fire. He then pointed it into the air, pulled the trigger and it fired. Shortly afterwards he wrote in a letter: 'It seems that fate must be saving me for some purpose'.

His name as a fighter was made in November 1751. With a force of only 240 men, Clive was able to capture the French fortress at Arcot. Then they fought off a much larger French counter-attack. He won a reputation for being a lucky commander, who took big risks.

A One of his Indian allies, Muhammed Ali, wrote to him in 1751:

> By God Almighty's grace you are very lucky in all your battles. Fortune is bent in your favour.

Shortly afterwards Clive married and returned to England. He was now a rich man. He did not return to India until the outbreak of war in Bengal.

In 1756 the 19-year-old Siraj ud Daulah succeeded as Nawab of Bengal. In June 1756 Siraj decided to drive the British out of Bengal, and his forces captured the main British base there, Calcutta.

One of the most controversial events of the century followed. Siraj imprisoned the Europeans he had captured. A very large number of them died on the night they were captured. Exactly how they died is the question.

They were all put in a tiny cell which usually housed five or six people. It was known as the 'black hole'. We have no account of what happened written by any Indian witnesses. The only account we have of what happened next was written by a survivor, Zephaniah Holwell. He was the Acting Commander in Calcutta.

Holwell wrote that 145 men and one woman spent from 8 pm on 20 June 1756 to 6 am the following morning there. The temperature was over 45 degrees centigrade. When they were released only 22 men and the woman, Mary Carey, were still alive. This incident was used back in Britain to show that Britain's enemies were savages. But what really happened?

B A drawing of 'The Black Hole of Calcutta', done in England, probably in 1757. It was meant to stir public feelings about the war in India.

C This is Holwell's version:

When the prisoners were thrown in, I requested silence while I spoke to them. I assured them that the return of day would give us air and liberty, that the only chance of surviving the night was the preserving of a calm mind.

Most of the guards were off celebrating their victory. Holwell tried to get the remaining guards to tell the Nawab that they were suffering, but the guards were frightened to wake him.

D Before 9 o'clock every man's thirst grew intolerable. Think, if possible, what my heart must have suffered at seeing their distress, without having it in my power to help them. I begged that they allow me to reach the window to die in quiet. I travelled over the dead.

Holwell only survived the night by drinking his own urine and sweat. Early the next morning the prisoners were let out. Holwell was threatened that he would be shot dead if he did not tell where the garrison's money was. He did not know. Eventually Siraj burnt down Calcutta and at the end of June the surviving European prisoners were set free.

Holwell wrote his account of what had happened to him on the way back to England, where it became a best seller. It was the start of a new career for Holwell as a successful author. He then campaigned to be made governor of Bengal. He eventually succeeded and had a very successful career in the East India Company too.

Modern Indians have denied these stories. They say that Holwell exaggerated for personal reasons and for war propaganda. In times of war, people and governments often tell lies about the enemy, to make it easier to hate them. These lies are called propaganda.

E In 1966 the Indian historian B.K. Gupta re-examined the facts and claimed that:

64 people were imprisoned, of whom 21 survived.

Gupta argued that Holwell increased the numbers by including people who had already been killed in the fighting when Calcutta was captured.

Clive recaptured what was left of Calcutta without a battle in January 1757. He then defended it against further attacks from Siraj.

Clive saw that he now had a chance to take Bengal for Britain. He formed an alliance with one of Siraj's generals, Mir Jafar, and defeated Siraj at

the battle of Plassey (see pages 50-1).

Clive's final campaign was in 1763, when he put the seal on British rule in Bengal. This last campaign was the most bitterly fought of all. At the main battle, Baksar, (at which Clive was not present) the British lost 847 out of 7,000 men. These were terrible losses for an 18th-century battle.

F After Baksar Clive wrote to the Chairman of the East India Company:

The whole Mughal empire is now in our hands. We must become the rulers, in fact if not in name. I am determined to return to England, without one penny addition to my fortune.

Before he left India Clive signed the Treaty of Allahabad with the Mughal emperor, Shah Alam. This did indeed make the British the real rulers of the Mughal empire.

G The signing of the Treaty of Allahabad.

Holwell's is the only account of the 'Black Hole' incident written by anyone involved in it.

1 Does that mean that it is certain to be true? Give reasons for your answer.

2 a) How did Holwell benefit personally from the incident?
b) Does this affect his reliability as a witness?

3 If you could interview others connected with the incident, whom would you choose? Give reasons for your choice.

4 How reliable as evidence is the 1757 picture (source B)? Give reasons.

5 'We can never know the full truth about the Black Hole of Calcutta'.
a) What does this statement mean?
b) Do you agree? Give reasons.

THE BATTLE OF PLASSEY

| 1400 | 1500 | 1600 | 1700 | 1800 | 1900 |

A battle is confusing. No one can see or know everything that is happening. It is sometimes difficult to decide why one side won and the other lost. Even so, a historian has to try and find causes and put the causes into an order of importance.

Plassey was the battle that made the British rulers of Bengal. This meant that, in effect, they ruled all of northern India.

While Clive was talking with Siraj about compensation money to rebuild Calcutta, he was also secretly plotting with Siraj's general, Mir Jafar.

In early June 1757 Clive left Calcutta with 800 European and 2,200 Indian troops. They marched 80 miles north towards Siraj's camp at Plassey. Siraj had over 40,000 men, French military advisers and artillery. If Clive was to win he had to be sure that Mir Jafar would at least keep his men out of the battle. Clive hoped that Mir Jafar and his troops might even fight alongside the British. So he kept sending coded messages to Mir Jafar, trying to get a promise from him, but without success.

A Clive's code system.

B Clive wrote to Mir Jafar on 14 June:
Come over to me at Plassey or any other place you judge proper, with what force you have. I prefer conquering by open force.

But he got no reply. He feared that Mir Jafar might have changed his mind, or even told Siraj about the plot.

On 21 June Clive met his officers to decide what to do. Ten voted to return to Calcutta without a fight. Five voted to attack, as did Clive. After thinking it over in private for an hour, Clive ordered an attack.

C The following day Mir Jafar at last answered:
When you come near I shall then be able to join you.

23 June 1757 began bright and sunny. Clive's forces were based near a river. Nearby was a grove of mango trees, which gave them some protection. To the north, near two water storage-tanks, were 50 French troops with four cannon. Siraj brought his men to face the British in a vast semi-circle: 35,000 footsoldiers, 8,000 cavalry and 53 cannon.

D Luke Scrafton was a British officer. He wrote:
What with the number of elephants, all covered in scarlet, their horses with drawn swords glittering in the sun, their cannon drawn by vast train of oxen, they made a most formidable sight.

The battle began at 8 a.m., with both sides firing their cannon and an Indian cavalry charge which the British defeated. A lucky British shot killed one of Siraj's generals. But there was still no sign that Mir Jafar was going to switch sides as promised.

At noon everything came to a total halt when an enormous thunderstorm soaked everyone. The British were able to keep their gunpowder dry. The Indians and French were not. Their guns were put out of action.

What happened next is unclear. At 3 p.m. Siraj began to pull back his forces. No one knows why he did this. He may have found out about Mir Jafar's plot. He may have lost his nerve or been worried about the wet gunpowder.

a	19	15	b
b	15	16	l
c	27	17	x
d	30	18	h
e	20	19	a
f	39	20	e
g	28	21	&
h	18	22	w
i	38	23	o
k	33	24	t
l	16	25	p
m	29	26	y
n	32	27	c
o	23	28	g
p	25	29	m
q	37	30	d
r	34	31	s
s	31	32	n
t	24	33	k
u	35	34	r
w	22	35	u
x	17	36	z
y	26	37	q
z	36	38	i
&	21	39	f

E Khulam Husain, a Bengali writer who was there, said:

> Siraj was told that his troops were deserting. Fearing not just the English, but more the traitors on his own side, he lost all firmness of mind and joined the deserters himself.

At that moment a British officer, Major Kilpatrick, launched an attack, without Clive's permission. This attack turned the Indian retreat into panic. Siraj got onto a camel and fled. His troops followed, scattering in all directions.

By 5 p.m. it was all over. British losses were tiny: four European and 14 Indian troops killed; nine Europeans and 36 Indians wounded. The losses on the other side are not recorded. Things had not gone according to anyone's plans. Mir Jafar had not switched sides, but he had not fought for Siraj either. Kilpatrick's charge had won the day. But Clive was angry that he had charged without permission. Clive said that he would have put Kilpatrick on trial if he had not won the battle!

Siraj was hunted down by Mir Jafar's son and hacked to death. He was 20 years old and had ruled Bengal for only 15 months.

F That evening Clive sent this message to the Company's officials in Calcutta:

> This morning we arrived at Plassey. The nawab's army fired at us for several hours. We advanced and stormed the nawab's camp. We have taken all his cannon and pursued him six miles. Mir Jafar gave us no assistance other than standing neutral. Our loss is trifling.

The next day Mir Jafar came to meet Clive. He was nervous about how Clive would welcome him, but Clive gave him a warm welcome. Mir Jafar was going to be the new Nawab of Bengal. But it was made clear to him that the real rulers would now be the British East India Company.

G As Clive wrote, to the Company's Directors, on 26 July:

> The day after the battle Mir Jafar paid me a visit. He expressed gratitude at the service done to him, and assured me that he would faithfully keep his promises to the English.

H This painting shows the meeting of Clive and Mir Jafar. The British government put it on display in London to make people feel patriotic during the Seven Years War.

1 Work in pairs.
a) List all the causes you can think of why Clive won and Siraj lost.
b) Then try to put them into an order, starting with the most important cause and ending with the least important.

c) Then compare your list with others in the class. Can the class agree about what were the three most important reasons for Clive's victory and Siraj's defeat?

2 Which of the sources in this chapter is the most useful in helping us to understand what happened at Plassey? Give reasons.

The East India Company did not set out to conquer India. Its aim was to make money. But as the Company brought more and more land under its control, it had to start being a government as well as a business. By the end of the century the East India Company ruled an area as big as the Mughal empire had been.

A India at the end of the 18th century.

The few thousand British in India could not possibly rule such a big area alone. Instead they worked out a system called 'indirect rule'. This was first tried by Clive, when he made Mir Jafar the new ruler of Bengal.

It worked like this. As far as possible Indian rulers were kept in place, still rich and respected. They took care of all the day-to-day running of the country. But it would all be a sham. They would really be puppets. Behind every Indian ruler would be a British 'adviser' who would tell the ruler what to do. Rulers who disobeyed their British advisers did not last very long.

Even the Mughal emperor became a British puppet. In 1784 Emperor Shah Alam II was taken prisoner by Indian rebels, who blinded him. From then on he ruled little more than the Red Fort in Delhi. Finally, in 1803, the Wellesley brothers brought Delhi itself under British control.

B Richard Wellesley described the wretched Emperor Shah Alam II, as he was found by the British troops.

> . . . old, without power, suffering from extreme poverty and loss of sight, seated under a small tattered canopy , which was all that was left of his royal state.

For ordinary Indians – the millions of peasants who lived in India's villages – life became worse under the East India Company. The Company kept in power the zamindars, the officials who had run the Mughal empire. The zamindars collected rents from the peasants.

These rents were higher than ever. This was because a percentage of the rent now had to go the the Company, as well as some to the Indian ruler and to the zamindar. As the Indian princes and the zamindar were not going to take a cut, the extra money could only be found by squeezing more out of the peasants.

In the 18th and 19th centuries there was an 'agricultural revolution' in Britain. British farms were the most advanced in the world. British rule had the opposite effect in India. The Company kept greedy money-lenders and landlords in power, while peasants were crushed by poverty, taxes and debt.

Before the East India Company took over.

After the East India Company took over.

Everyone agreed that India was full of bribery and corruption while it was ruled by the Company. Time and again the Company tried to reform itself. In 1786, Lord Cornwallis took over as Governor General, determined to clean up the Indian administration.

C Cornwallis said at the time:
Every native of India, I truly believe, is corrupt.

The first thing that he did was sack every single Indian employed by the Company. But there is no evidence at all that this did any good.

D A cartoon from 1772, showing the guilty directors of the East India Company being haunted by the ghosts of their Indian victims.

Parliament had become worried about how the Company was running India. In 1784 the India Act gave Parliament the right to oversee what the Company was doing. Every 20 years the Company would have to apply to get its charter renewed. (The charter made it illegal for anyone else to trade with India.)

The Company directors were not happy but had no choice. Unusually, the early 1780s were bad for the Company. It actually made a loss. It had to ask the government for a £1 million loan.

Prime Minister William Pitt said that if it wanted the loan it would have to give up some of its independence to Parliament. So it got the loan but had to take the India Act too. In 1793 the Company had to apply to Parliament for the first time to have its charter renewed.

Two groups campaigned against the renewal of the charter. One was made up of businessmen. They said that it was unfair to have only one company allowed to trade with India. They wanted free trade. The other group was made up of Christians. The Company had always banned Christian missionaries, to avoid trouble with Indian rulers who were not Christians.

E An Indian wooden model showing an official of the East India Company running a court.

The Company spent a lot of money buying friends in Parliament. Luckily for it, war with France started in 1793. With a war on, Parliament decided not to make risky changes. The East India Company got its charter renewed.

Twenty years later the Christians and the Free Traders had grown in influence. This time the East India Company lost. In 1813, after 213 years, the Company lost the right to be the only British company trading in India. Trade with India was open to everyone.

Of course, the Company kept enormous powers. It ran a huge empire in India, with its own army and navy. But it was now more like a branch of the British government, responsible for ruling India.

1 How was British rule in India (a) like Mughal rule and (b) unlike Mughal rule?

2 It is the year 1793. Parliament is deciding whether or not to renew the East India Company's charter. Write three letters to Parliament.
- (1) is from the East India Company itself, saying what a great job it has done and why it should carry on as before.
- (2) is from a businessman who wants to trade directly with India but cannot because of the East India Company. You think that this is unfair and that it leads to the Company charging too much.
- (3) is from William Wilberforce, who strongly believes that the East India Company is wrong to keep Christian missionaries out of India. You oppose renewing the charter.

HOW THE BRITISH LIVED IN INDIA

A A description of the behaviour of Europeans in the English colony of Madras, by an English chaplain , 1676.

Some are murderers, some are stealers, some are Catholics, some have their wives in England and here live in adultery. Others pride themselves on making others drink until they are senseless and then strip them naked and cause them to be carried through the streets to their dwelling place. Some of them once drank all day and night, so much that one of them died!

The Englishmen who went to India to work for the East India Company did not go there to teach the Indians European ways and beliefs. They went to make money. The East India Company was happy to leave Indians to their own ways of life. For example, it banned Christian missionaries from working in its territories throughout the 18th century, to avoid upsetting Hindus and Muslims.

Many wealthy English merchants, who were nicknamed nabobs , married into Indian noble families. They adopted Indian dress and food, smoked Indian pipes and learned to speak Indian languages. They did this partly because there were few upper-class Englishwomen in India. If men wanted a family and social life they had to fit into Indian society. Back in England, this behaviour was regarded as strange and even evil.

There seems to have been very little racism in the attitudes of the English towards the Indians in the 18th century. It was not until Victorian times that the English started to think that they were superior to the Indians.

Source B shows a durbar, or audience with an Indian prince, held in 1790. The Englishmen shown seem happy to sit at the feet of an Indian prince and to respect Indian customs.

Rich servants of the Company could live a life of luxury. An English visitor to India claimed that this was a typical day for an English merchant in Bengal in the 1780s:

C James Mackintosh: *Travels in Europe and Africa* (1783).

In the morning his clothes are put upon his body as if he were a statue. While his hairdresser prepares his hair he eats, sips and smokes. He leaves for work at ten and at two sits down to dinner with a party of friends. At four he goes to his bedroom where he sleeps. He rises at seven or eight and may make some visits, returning for supper. His guests may stay until midnight. After they leave he is conducted to his bedroom where he finds a female companion to amuse him until dawn. With no greater efforts than these, the Company's servants make the most splendid fortunes.

B The Poona Durbar of 1790.

D Robert Clive himself described this life in a speech in Parliament:

Flesh and blood cannot bear the temptations which are put in the way of the newly-arrived Englishman. Others, arrived only a year before him, have fine houses of their own, ride upon prancing arabian horses, keep Indian women, drink champagne and claret.

The number of men rich enough to lead such a life would have been quite small. There were fewer than 40,000 Englishmen in India at any time in the 18th century. Of these, about 3,000 worked for the East India Company as traders. Then there were about 6,000 officers in the company's army. The rest were common soldiers.

E Sir David Ochterlony, the senior British official in Delhi, at a party in his house, 1820.

This illustration suggests that some of the British still adopted Indian ways as late as 1820. But by the early 19th century this was no longer the rule. There were three big changes:

● The first was the arrival in India of large numbers of British women, from around the 1760s. Robert Clive, for example, married the sister of a friend. She was visiting her brother in India. From this time, fewer Englishmen mixed with Indians in their social life. Fewer married or lived with Indian women. Instead the British had their own, separate society.

● Secondly, the British began to feel themselves superior to Indians. This may be because they saw that India was falling into poverty, while Britain had become the richest country in the world.

● Thirdly, British exports were now widely available in India, for those who could afford to buy them. The British could keep up the lifestyle they had enjoyed back home.

F The Emporium of Taylor & Co. in Calcutta, 1825, by Sir Charles D'Oyly.

This exclusive shop catered for the wives of British officers in Bengal in the early 19th century. Its owners boasted that there was nothing available in London's shops which they could not supply.

G Sir Charles D'Oyly described this shop in a poem which he wrote in 1824:

Of every tasteful article a store,
On tables heaped reveal their varied charms.

There was a campaign in Britain in the 18th century to prove that the English in India were leading wicked lives. Partly this came from Christians who were angry that the East India Company refused to allow missionaries into its lands. Partly it was jealously of the wealth and power of the nabobs like Robert Clive who came back to England. Remember this when answering the questions.

1 Why were people in England jealous of the nabobs?
2 a) Sources A and C take a certain attitude towards the English in India. Describe this attitude, with some examples.
   b) How useful does that make these comments as sources of historical information?
3 a) Does the statement by Robert Clive (source D) support or deny the statement by Mackintosh (source C)?
   b) Does that make it more or less likely that Mackintosh is truthful? Give reasons.
4 When source C was published in Britain what might the response have been?

| 1400 | 1500 | 1600 | 1700 | 1800 | 1900 |

Only one person in this book is in the *Guinness Book of Records*. Warren Hastings was one of the great Governors General of the East India Company. But he is remembered now for a court case. In one of the longest cases in history, he was accused of greed, cruelty and corruption. It is surprising that Hastings ended in court. He had been sent to 'clean up' India.

There was a lot of talk about India in Britain. Some people believed that the British in India were not firm enough. The prejudice caused by the 'black hole of Calcutta' incident took a long time to go away.

In Britain some said the East India Company was greedy. The directors decided they needed to clean up their act. Hastings took over in 1772.

He did do some good. A new system of courts of justice was set up. Tax collection was made simpler. It was made harder for people to steal from the Company or from the people of India. Hastings won wars against the French in India. He valued Indian culture. He could speak Urdu, Bengali and Farsi and he paid for the first English translation of the Hindu holy books.

But there were danger signs. Hastings involved the Company in the drugs trade. Opium had been grown and used in India for centuries. It was legal but people knew how dangerous it was.

B Hastings knew what he was doing. He said:
Opium is an evil thing. The wisdom of the Company will not allow it to be sold in the areas it rules.

But he allowed opium to be widely grown in British India and to be sold all over the East.

What really got Hastings into trouble was a complicated legal case. A businessman called Nandkumar accused Hastings of taking bribes. Soon after, Nandkumar himself was charged with forging money, found guilty and hanged.

It was the first time anyone in India had been executed for forgery. The judge in the case was a school friend of Hastings. Hastings had made him Chief Justice. As Governor General, Hastings could have pardoned Nandkumar. He did not. It was all *very* suspicious.

Hastings' enemies returned to England and spread stories against him. There were plenty to listen. Many were sick of the power and wealth of the nabobs who ruled India. Some were ashamed of what had been done there. They saw the Company getting rich while Bengal starved.

A This cartoon from 1770 shows Englishmen being ill-treated by Indians, while the East India Company, represented by Robert Clive, does nothing. (Some Englishmen are shown as animals to imply that they are stupid and deserve what they get.)

C The trial of Warren Hastings, Westminster Hall, 13 February 1788.

One of Hastings' fiercest critics was Edmund Burke. Even his enemies agreed that Burke was the best speechmaker in Britain. He spoke in Parliament, demanding that Hastings be put on trial.

In 1785 Hastings came home. He brought back £80,000, a small amount compared to what some Englishmen made in India.

He felt that he had done a good job in India.

D On the ship he wrote in his journal:
I have saved India, in spite of them all, from foreign conquest.

His enemies were waiting. In 1788 Hastings was put on trial before the House of Lords, charged with corruption and cruelty. Burke spoke for the prosecution.

E Burke said:
I am speaking in the name of the Indian people, whose rights Hastings has trodden under foot, whose country he has turned into a desert.

F Burke went back to the Nandkumar case:
Nandkumar was hanged in the face of all his nation, insulting everything which India holds sacred, hanged by the judges that we sent to protect the Indian people, hanged for a pretend crime.

The case was a big event. Thousands queued to see one of the most important men in the world on trial. Tourists even came over from France.

G One eye-witness was Madame d'Arblay. She wrote:
The left side of the hall was for Lords and their daughters. The bottom of the hall contained the Royal Family's box. The Queen and four princesses were there. I shuddered. What an awful moment for such a man!

The trial went on and on. Burke could not prove Hastings guilty and Hastings could not prove that he was innocent. Finally, after *7 years*, Hastings was found Not Guilty. It did him little good. His legal costs were £100,000. He was £20,000 in debt. Hastings lived until 1818. He got a small pension but died a very poor man.

---

1 This chapter contains information showing that English people in the 1780s had divided views about India and about the East India Company. What evidence is there to support each of these statements?
- People thought that the Company was robbing India.
- People thought that the Company was too soft.
- People thought that all the problems in India were Hastings' fault.
- People thought that Hastings was being blamed for other people's crimes and were sorry for him.

The same person can be seen very differently depending on your point of view. To friends and supporters they might be good while their enemies can see only the harm that they do. This chapter looks at such a man: Tipu Sultan, nicknamed the Tiger of Mysore.

A A modern Indian writer, B. S. Gidwani, recently wrote:

Tipu Sultan was the only Indian ruler of the 18th century who did not side with the English at *any* time in a war with his fellow countrymen.

Tipu Sultan was one of the bitterest enemies of the British in India. For this reason he was seen as evil by the British. But, to modern Indians like B. S. Gidwani, Tipu is a hero. There is a popular television series based upon his life, 'The Sword of Tipu Sultan'.

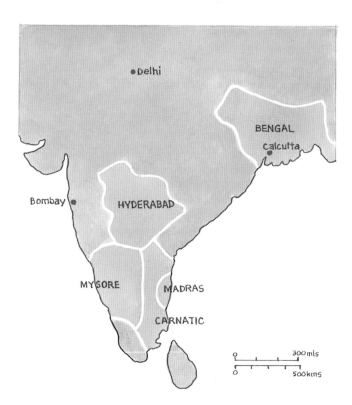

B Map of the areas mentioned in this chapter.

Tipu's father Haidar had seized the throne of Mysore. He then sided with the French to try to drive the British out of southern India. In 1780 Haidar inflicted a heavy defeat on the British. They were driven from the Carnatic and it looked as if Madras itself might fall. However, the Governor General, Warren Hastings, kept his nerve and at the battle of Porto Novo, near Madras, Haidar Ali was beaten.

Haidar died soon after. His son Tipu had played a leading role in his father's war, leading units of cavalry. He had seen that the British could be beaten by his father. He decided to do the same himself.

In 1789 Tipu attacked. Again the British were forced to fall back to Madras. Lord Cornwallis, the Governor General of the East India Company, came in person from Calcutta to lead the counter-attack. Cornwallis formed an alliance with the Nizam of Hyderabad, a powerful Indian ruler who was worried by Tipu's new power.

In 1791 they attacked Tipu but Tipu beat them off. In 1792 they returned and this time Tipu was forced to surrender. He had to pay a huge fine and to give up large areas of his kingdom.

C Still from the television series 'The Sword of Tipu Sultan'.

D Cornwallis wrote:
We are forced into the war by Tipu's uncontrollable ambition and the violence of his character.

To ensure that Tipu did not break the treaty, his two sons were taken away as hostages for two years by the British.

Neither Tipu nor the British saw this as the end. In 1793 war began between Britain and France. This was a good time for Tipu to act. He made contact with the French. In 1798 the French army, led by general Napoleon Bonaparte, invaded Egypt. Tipu hoped that the French would win there and push on to India. That would be his chance to drive the British out of India for good.

Tipu told the French government that he supported the French Revolution and allowed them to call him 'Citizen Tipu'. A small French force was sent to help him.

E This is from an Indian comic book about Tipu.

However, it was the new British Governor General, Richard Wellesley, who hit first. Mysore was invaded by the British in 1798. Tipu was trapped in his fortress at Seringapatam and a long seige followed. The attack on the fortress was led by Wellesley's younger brother, Arthur, who later became the Duke of Wellington. Tipu was killed in the final attack on the fort.

The British gave Tipu a hero's funeral with full honours. It was very dramatic. As it took place, there was a huge thunderstorm in which two British officers were killed by lightning. Many Indians saw this as an act of God.

But Tipu's sons were barred from becoming king and forced to leave Mysore. A treaty was signed with a new ruler, who had been put in power by the British.

Now Mysore would be '*protected*' by the East India Company and would pay the Company £280,000 each year for this 'protection'. The Company could also interfere as much as it liked in

the affairs of Mysore. In short, Mysore was under complete British rule. Arthur Wellesley, the new Governor of Seringapatam, was its real ruler.

There is no doubt that Tipu and the British hated each other. When Mysore was conquered a lifesize wooden carving was found in Tipu's palace. It was made for Tipu's entertainment. It shows a tiger killing an English soldier. Inside is a clockwork mechanism. When it is wound up the tiger growls and the soldier screams!

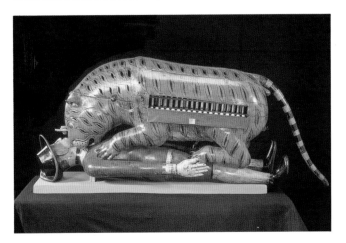

F Tipu's tiger.

The English believed that Tipu was very cruel to prisoners and that he refused to release them when he had said that he would. Modern British historians believe this was so the prisoners could train his troops to use the latest equipment.

Tipu claimed that the men he kept were not just prisoners of war. He said that they had robbed from his people and should be treated as criminals.

A modern Indian point of view is shown in source E. Tipu was respected by all the Indian people of Mysore. Although he was a Muslim, he was popular with the many Hindus that he ruled. He is still held in honour in India.

___

1　Are the sources (a) from the comic and (b) from the television series primary or secondary evidence? Give reasons.
2　Why might a historian today be interested in popular TV shows and stories from modern India about Tipu?
3　This chapter contains information both 'for' and 'against' Tipu. Use examples from this chapter to show that different people can hold very different views about the same person.
4　After reading this chapter, do you think that it is possible for a historian to be fair about an enemy after his death?

CHANGE AND CONTINUITY

After the British took Delhi in 1803, the last traces of the power of the Mughals were gone. Britain now ruled northern and southern India. The Marathas were still strong in the centre of India. And the Sikh king, Ranjit Singh, ruled Punjab. But British rule in India was almost complete.

The Mughals still lasted for another 55 years, now called the *Kings of Delhi*. But they had no power at all. They were paid a pension by the British government as long as they kept out of politics.

A This is Bahadur Shah II, the last of the Mughals, painted in 1838. The writing on the picture gives some of his titles: 'God's Shadow upon the Earth', 'The King of Kings', 'Refuge of the Nations', 'The Protector of Islam'. These titles all date back to the 16th century. They had once suited Babur, Akbar and Jahangir. They did not really fit a man who ruled only the palace where he lived.

Bahadur Shah was not a fool and he understood the sad position that he was in. He was a well-known poet and wrote:

B All that I have loved is gone:
Like a garden.
Robbed of its Beauty by Autumn.
I am only a memory of splendour.

In the early 19th century Delhi and nearby Mughal cities like Agra were popular sights for British visitors to India. They were curious to see what was left of the Mughal empire, especially its great buildings. The Taj Mahal, Shah Jahan's tomb for Mumtaz Mahal, had become dirty and damaged. It was restored and made into India's top tourist attraction. It was fashionable for British artists to paint sad pictures of romantic Mughal ruins.

C A Delhi fort, built by Humayun, painted in 1823.

The Mughal empire had lasted at full strength for almost 190 years. During the 18th century it was replaced by other Indian rulers – the Marathas, the Sikhs, Bengal, Mysore. In their turn these were defeated by the British.

The British government had not set out to conquer India. The India Act of 1784 actually made it *illegal* for the East India Company to interfere in Indian politics. By then it was too late. The officials of the Company in India were already well on the way to ruling the whole country.

Many British people felt proud of what they had done. They looked forward to India enjoying a great future under British rule. Many changes were under way. One big change was the spread of English education and the English language.

This photograph from 1890 shows the machine room of the *Times of India* (an Indian newspaper, written in English for Indian readers). European industry, European ideas, European values and the English language were all going to have a big impact upon India. Many Indians learnt English and came to England for education. Today English is still one of the official languages of India.

But India's traditional culture did survive. Despite the work of Christian missionaries, both Hinduism and Islam remained strong. The only part of India which became Christian was Goa, where the Portuguese had always allowed Christian missionaries to work.

In fact there was a big rebirth of Hinduism in the 19th century. This began in Bengal, the part of India which had suffered most from British rule. In 1809 the Kalighat, the temple of the Hindu Mother Goddess in Calcutta, was rebuilt. It became the most popular temple in India. Millions visited it every year. By the end of the century Hinduism was stronger than ever before, especially in Bengal. And it was again in Bengal that the movements to win independence for India began.

E   Painting of the Kalighat, 1873.

And British rule did not solve the problems of hunger and poverty in India's countryside. Source F was drawn by an unknown artist in 1840, during a famine. During the 1830s and 1840s hunger killed millions of people in India.

The British might have expected that their rule in India would last for ever. Many ordinary Indians did not. There was a popular saying that it would only last for 100 years from the Battle of Plassey. If British rule is dated from Plassey, in 1757, then it lasted for almost exactly the same time as Mughal rule: 190 years.

In 1857 there was a huge rebellion against British rule, usually known as the Indian Mutiny. It must have seemed that the prediction was coming true. The rebels tried to make Bahadur Shah II a real emperor again. They were defeated, but it shook the British government so badly that the East India Company was abolished. Bahadur Shah was kept as a prisoner outside India until he died. Then Queen Victoria became Empress of India.

In the 19th century Britain built one of the biggest empires that had ever existed. India was at its heart, the 'jewel in the crown'. Indians were encouraged by the British government to leave home and seek work in other parts of the British empire. Some went as soldiers. The British army had hundreds of thousands of Indian troops. Others went as labourers, as merchants or as students. By the end of the 19th century there were large Indian communities across the world – in Britain, Singapore, South Africa, Canada, Fiji, Trinidad and many other countries. (See the map on page 62.)

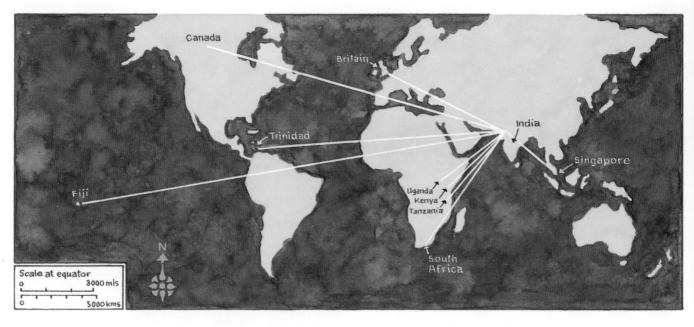

G The Indian community across the world.

But most Indians had not given up hope of one day ruling themselves. From 1905 they began demanding 'Home Rule' for India. They could look back to the glories of the Mughal empire, to Shivaji and Tipu Sultan. These great examples gave them hope and self-confidence. The two men who led India's struggle to rule itself – Mohandas Gandhi and Jawaharlal Nehru – had both been students in Britain. They believed British rule could be ended without violence, if Indians did not pay British taxes, buy British goods or obey unjust laws. They believed that the British people could be made to see that they should not be ruling India.

In 1947 the British ended their rule in India. Two new independent states, India and Pakistan, were created from former British India. Finally, in 1961, the Indian army took back the Portuguese colony of Goa. The Portuguese had been the first Europeans to arrive and they were the last to go.

1 Why did the Hindu revival and the Indian independence movement start in *Bengal*, rather than in any other part of India?

2 In pairs, divide a page into two columns. On the left put **different.** On the right **similar.** Then compare this chapter with the first two chapters of the book. Over the 300 years some things in India changed a lot and some things hardly changed at all.

  On the left side of your page write those things which had changed in India over this time. Number each one. On the right put the things which remained the same. Number each one.

3 a) Now compare your lists with the others in the class.
  b) Are there more items under different or under similar?
  c) Does your answer to (b) tell us anything about India's history?

H Gandhi at 10 Downing Street in 1931.

I Nehru became India's first prime minister in 1947.

GLOSSARY

ambassador – a person who represents his or her country's government in another country

astronomy – the study of the stars

autobiography – a person's life story, told by themselves

bankrupt – having no money left

bigotry – not respecting the views of others

bombard – to hit with cannon fire

canopy – a cloth shelter

census – count of how many people there are in a country

chaplain – a Christian religious minister

charter – an official document which sets up a company

chronological – in the order in which the events happened

civil war – when the people of one country fight each other

colours – regimental flag

cremation yards – places where corpses are burnt

culture – the traditional way of life of a people

decline – slow failure

descendant – person who is descended from you (eg your child, grandchild)

dynasty – royal family

exile – forced to live away from your home, usually in a foreign country

fakir – a wandering holy man or other beggar

famine – when thousands of people starve

fanatic – a person who thinks that his or her ideas are the only ones that matter

guerilla war – war of surprise attacks and raids

hostage – person held as a prisoner so that someone else will be forced to do a deal for his or her freedom

independent – ruling themselves, not ruled by another

inherited – gained a person's property when they died

invading – entering another country as an enemy

journal – diary

logic – the study of how to think clearly

martyr – a person who dies because of what he or she believes in

missionaries – people who go to another country to spread their religion

mosque – a building where Muslims meet to pray

mullah – a Muslim religious leader

nabob – nickname for an Englishman who made his fortune in India

nawab – an Indian prince

nobility – the people who owned land

patriotic – loving one's own country

physiognomy – understanding a person's character from his or her face

pilgrimage – a visit to a holy place

prejudiced – having a closed mind to other people's points of view

prophet – a person who is believed by his or her followers to have been sent by God

ramparts – walls of a castle

recruit – to hire soldiers

stature – height

vibrated – shook backwards and forwards very quickly to make a noise

INDEX